D1426030

MW
Đ20
MW
CEAR
95000506

IOC Ocean Forum I

Coastal zone space
Prelude to conflict?

Edward D. Goldberg
Scripps Institution of Oceanography
La Jolla, California 92093 USA

Environment and Development

UNESCO Publishing

Published in 1994
by the United Nations Educational,
Scientific and Cultural Organization,
7 place de Fontenoy, 75352 Paris 07 SP

Composed by Susanne Almeida-Klein
Printed by Imprimerie de la Manutention, 53100 Mayenne

ISBN 92-3-102953-3

Preface

Agenda 21 adopted by the United Nations Conference on Environment and Development (UNCED) in Rio de Janeiro, in June 1992, sets out a number of concerns and 'critical uncertainties' that must be addressed urgently by societies and governments concerning the environment and the sustainable development of our planet's resources. One of these concerns is the future of coastal zones and areas, and integrated coastal zone management is highlighted as a need. The present book explores several facets (including practical, technical and cultural aspects) of the problems facing this vital strip of our Earth where an often heavily populated and exploited land and coastal marine area joins the as yet more virgin deep ocean.

In presenting this volume to the international community, the Intergovernmental Oceanographic Commission (IOC) of UNESCO seeks to fulfil one of the Organization's basic mandates: to serve as a world forum for the exchange of ideas and information that will provide decision-makers with the factual, scientific basis and other arguments upon which to establish relevant policy and legislation. Also in line with the spirit of UNCED, the Commission, in its area of competence, supports a call for a broader environmental education towards a more enlightened world citizenry.

Professor Edward D. Goldberg is a well-known author and speaker on the subject matter of this book. The present text not only reviews the developments and revelations which have transpired particularly since the publication of his *The Health of the Oceans* (UNESCO, 1976), but also addresses a set of questions previously not evident to the world community on such a wide scale.

In his treatment of the problems, the author selects certain alternatives, presenting the advantages and dangers of each and where relevant indicating his recommended option. Background information and arguments are given in digested, readable form whereas, for the more curious reader, the references at the end of each chapter provide a wealth of carefully selected sources of information on the subject. The volume demonstrates Professor Goldberg's capacity to look at the global issues from several points of view, ranging from cultural, legal and social science to scientific and technical considerations.

Other than wishing to provide a forum for discussion through the medium of the series, the Organization itself maintains a neutral position in the discussions that follow. The ideas, choice of materials and references, and any expressed or unexpressed proposals contained herein, are those of the author and do not engage the responsibility of the publisher, nor do they necessarily reflect opinions of UNESCO or its IOC.

Contents

Foreword

Robert B. Clark

Former editor, *Marine Pollution Bulletin*

Concern about the health of the global environment became fashionable in the 1980s and looks set to remain so for some time to come. It has become clear that the human population is capable of causing environmental damage on a regional or even global scale, and some avoiding action will have to be taken. It is always prudent to plan ahead, but to do so implies a knowledge, or at least a reasonable expectation, of what future circumstances will be like. Unhappily, prognostication is anything but an exact science.

In the optimistic nineteenth century, this did not matter very much. 'Progress' was regarded as inevitable, and if plans did not exactly work out, there was always a new frontier to cross and the opportunity to make a fresh start. In the more pessimistic late twentieth century, there is less confidence about the inevitability of progress and few opportunities for making a fresh start. We start from where we are now, carrying the legacy of the past with us, and we have to manage our affairs in such a way that the planet will continue to sustain (human) life in tolerable conditions.

This is an anthropocentric and minimalist objective. There are environmentalists who will be offended by it: they are egocentric and the welfare of the natural environment must, for them, be given first priority. To be sure, humans are part of the global ecosystem and if that goes, humans go with it. But the philosophy runs deeper than that: humans should live in harmony with nature and not exploit it.

This is a fine sentiment, but not one that is easy to put across to those living in the middle of Los Angeles or New York, who have only the most tenuous contact with any 'natural' environment; furthermore, it involves an element of wishful thinking. Whether we live in harmony with nature or not, there will, for example, always be wastes to dispose of and any method of waste disposal has some environmental cost. We should seek a waste disposal option that minimizes the environmental cost, but we should not be deluded into thinking that there will be no environmental bill to pay, to say nothing of the financial bill.

As to life continuing in tolerable conditions, it is unfortunately true that for three quarters of the world's population, the conditions are already less than that. Readers of this book are likely to be drawn from the other quarter who, whatever they may wish, are hardly likely to find it tolerable to be deprived of automobiles, telephones or the other appurtenances and conveniences of the developed world. However, since the affluent quarter is responsible, directly or indirectly, for much of the pressure on the natural environment, they may be able to make a substantial contribution to reducing it.

Whether or not they do so depends on the political will to make changes. Politicians in democracies are rarely far behind or far ahead of public perceptions for very long, but public perceptions are notoriously unreliable and we face a considerable job of enlightened public education. It would be nice to think we live in a rational society, but we do not. The usual public perception of the threat to human health and life from nuclear power generation is high, that of traffic accidents is low. The actual risks (Chernobyl notwithstanding) are overwhelmingly in the opposite direction. But if a substantial reduction in carbon dioxide emissions to counter the greenhouse effect is to be achieved, as has been accepted by the Europeans (though not yet the United States), a switch from fossil fuel to nuclear power generation seems the only realistic solution. Few people have come to terms with that equation. So it is with the solutions to other global eco-problems we may soon have to confront. If the problems prove to be as severe as pessimists predict, some very hard decisions will have to be taken.

Underlying these problems is the burgeoning growth of the human population. People require space, food, water and shelter as a minimum, and a good deal more if they aspire to something approaching the present living standards of the developed world. Even their basic needs cannot be satisfied without encroaching still further on the natural environment. A pessimist will despair, but the human population has been managing its environment to support a steadily increasing population for several millennia (the English landscape is almost entirely man-made).

The sea is perhaps our last frontier and we have shown little skill or urgency in its management. In the past, it always seemed a limitless resource. But both the sea and coastal lands have come under increasing pressure in the last fifty years and we can no longer afford the luxury of mistreating it. This book gives forward projections from where we are now to where we may be in a decade or two. The pressure on this environment will certainly increase and the need for wise management of it will become more and more pressing. To be forewarned of future trends is to be forearmed to take the necessary precautionary measures to avoid more environmental destruction, if we have the will to do so. The wisdom in this book provides guidelines for further thought. One can only hope that similar wisdom will be shown in developing a rational management of our seas and coastlines.

Introduction

The study

This volume is addressed to those engaged in managing the coastal marine environment in one way or another, either for the first time or on a continuing basis, and especially to those who will be involved with the inevitable changes in uses of space in the future. It is written in a way intended to be understandable by administrators, social scientists, natural scientists and most of all by the lay public. Its focus is the coastal zone, the narrow band of water and land where the oceans meet the continents. Its concern is to maintain or improve the resources there for a growing world population placing more and more stresses upon them. The strategy will be the identification of conflicts that will arise among the various users of the coastal zone, whether they seek economic profit, aesthetic enjoyment, the solution of problems that develop elsewhere, or recreation.

The priority issues will be approached by examples drawn both from the industrialized and industrializing worlds. No attempt is made to be exhaustive, a word often used as a synonym for exhausting. Instead, the 'for instance's have been chosen to elaborate upon arguments, not to seek the appearance of an encyclopaedic volume. However, in some cases to make a point a large number of examples are presented, especially with respect to the microbial contamination of coastlines throughout the world, or the widespread and increasing occurrences of red tides and algal blooms.

I have not attempted to compile a complete catalogue of research needs in coastal zone management. There are simply too many. Instead I have tried to point out a few areas in which some additional knowledge will make the process of management more effective. Some of the research needs identified by scientists and engineers have not reached the eyes or ears of government officials or environmentalists. And yet the latter groups have unusual powers in formulating legislation and public policies to improve coastal zone quality. Finally, it must be emphasized that sometimes problems perceived as being of great importance turn out to be non-problems. Hopefully, there is a small number of such herein.

There are continual outcries against the use of the oceans as waste space for societal discards. National and international policies are directed against the disposal of wastes in the seas. This mood contrasts with that of many scientists and engineers who emphasize that the oceans are underutilized in the acceptance of wastes while land resources, such as subterranean waters, are being contaminated through the inadequate husbandry of toxic discards. For this reason an extended assessment of marine waste disposal is included, on the assumption that rational activities will become commonplace in the next decades.

Finally, social and political changes in a nation can reorder the priorities in coastal space utilization. This has been exemplified in developments in the former USSR (Vartanov, 1991). In the post-World War II period of the 1970s and 1980s, military usage and the scientific and engineering research to support it had the highest priorities (Table I.1; Vartanov, 1991). The increasing demand for animal protein explains the dedication given to the living resources of the sea.

The protection of the coastal zone received minimal emphasis, especially in view of the great importance of economic development. This has become especially evident in the face of declining productivity.

Table I.1. Priorities in coastal space utilization and research in the former USSR (Vartanov, 1991)

Area of interest	1970s–1980s	2000*	2000**
Military objectives	1	7	2
Scientific research	2	3	3
Bioresources utilization	3	4 =	4
Harbour development	4	6	5
Mineral resources	5	4 =	1
Recreation and tourism	6	1	7
Environmental protection	7	2	6

* Assuming democratization and the development of a market economy.

** Assuming an authoritative regime and the development of a market economy.

To further complicate matters there has been political unrest where various republics have gained independence from the previously constituted USSR. Vartanov (1991) suggests that the acceptance of the responsibility for managing the coastal zone by the republics could lead to an improved ecological situation. Less dependency upon military demands and a greater control of the resources by the regions can contribute to a more rational use of the coastal zone. The rearrangement of priorities (Table I.1) directs attention to the economic potential of recreation and tourism.

The learning process

This volume had its origin in an invitation to lecture on 'People, Pollution and the Oceans' at a Conference on Human Demography and Natural Resources on 1–3 February 1989 under the auspices of the Hoover Institution on War, Revolution and Peace, Palo Alto, California (Goldberg, 1991). Up to this time I had given little thought to the demographic problems relating to the coastal zone. But I was quickly educated. I continued my involvement through an address on 'Future Uses of the Oceans: Conflicts and Challenges', as the tenth lecturer in the Environmental Studies Visiting Scholar Series, sponsored by the Institute of Environmental Studies at the University of North Carolina, Chapel Hill. I have spoken on this topic at Hanyang University in Seoul, the Republic of Korea, the University of Massachusetts in Boston, the Mansfield Center for Pacific Affairs Conference on Pacific Environmental Issues and News Media Coverage in Bozeman, Montana, the Fourth International Conference on Environmental Futures in Budapest, Hungary and the Second International Symposium on Coastal Ocean Space Utilization in Long Beach, California, USA. A digest of this volume appeared in 1993.

I learned of the rising maricultural and touristic activities making demands upon the resources of the coastal zone. I was stunned by the increases in ranching and farming of the sea over the past decades to such an extent that the livelihoods of a large number of fishermen are threatened. Similarly, I was amazed to learn that about 10 per cent of the fish, shellfish and algae which are taken from natural waters comes about from aquaculture. Although a substantial proportion of the fish is from farming in terrestrial waters, there is an ever-increasing crop of these products taken from the sea.

I was aware of the apprehension regarding the discharges of pathogens in domestic wastes to the coastal zone and consequential morbidities or mortalities from the consumption of seafood. I had not realized that the association of disease and exposure to tainted waters through recreational activities was weak. Yet the perception of a strong cause/effect relationship exists in the eyes of many. The economic impact upon tourism can be disastrous. Many of the developing countries may have their economies slowed down through perceptions of polluted swimming beaches and seafoods unsafe for consumption.

I was struck by some approximate yet revealing statistics on the contribution of tourism to the world economy. I learned that tourism accounts for somewhere between 5 and 10 per cent of the world's gross national product. I suspect, but cannot as yet document, that the coastal zone probably is involved with a substantial percentage of this figure.

There will be many conflicts among those seeking to exploit the resources of the coastal zone. Thus, it is crucial to be aware of the varied uses of this part of the marine environment, of their economic and social values, and of possible regulatory activities to preserve the resources.

But of greater consequence in my search for knowledge was the publication of two volumes on demographics in the coastal zone. The first considered 50 years of population change along the US coasts (Culliton et al., 1990) and the second, the environmental and economic changes accompanying demographic changes in the Mediterranean (Grenon and Batisse, 1989).

Culliton et al. (op. cit.) are primarily concerned with environmental changes as a result of a predicted increase in the US coastal population between 1960 and 2010. They suspect that many of the qualities that give rise to attracting people to the coastal zone will diminish. They voice concern about the rise in contamination of the marine environment as documented by the monitoring activities of the US National Ocean and Atmospheric Administration.

The Mediterranean study was far more ambitious. It sought future relationships between various components of the environment and the main sectors of economic activity. The environment was divided up into five components: the soil, inland waters, forests, the coasts and the sea. The economy was presumed to have five important parts: agriculture, industry, energy, tourism and transport. The future horizons of 2000 and 2025 were chosen and a number of models developed with differing assumptions as to population, growth, economic activity, etc.

The investigation of societal impacts upon the coastal zone should fall into the arena of geographers. I learned that problems involving the lands bordering the oceans are well-treated by these scholars (see, for example, Ruddle et al., 1988). However, they display little concern for the associated water resources and how they may be affected by practices on land. There are all too few exceptions to this trend.

Finally, the lands and waters of the coastal zone are the repositories for parts of our cultural heritage (World Bank, 1990). On land, buildings, art works and historical monuments are victims to pollution, primarily in the atmosphere, and to urbanization (World Bank, 1990). At sea, sunken ships and submerged buildings are often plundered by unscrupulous adventurers, with the loss of historical artefacts. Some societal constructs, once on land, are now under water. The more valuable marine cultural sites have been identified by UNESCO. Such parts of our heritage, if properly maintained, are very attractive to the local citizenry as well as to tourists.

The diminishing coastal zone

There are impediments to the potential or extended use of the coastal zone through activities on land. For example, the cut-off in the supply of beach sand is the primary cause of coastal erosion (Inman, D. L. 'Dammed rivers and eroded coasts', Unpubl. ms., 1989). The loss of beaches for their recreational and aesthetic values may be reflected in decreased tourist revenue and in the overall quality of life for the resident citizenry. The problem to a large extent is the result of dams which result in the accumulation of the sand on the continents, sand which normally would have been fed by rivers to the oceans.

The northern Nile delta region is sinking and tilting toward the Mediterranean (*Science,* 1990). This is a result of the overlying weight of sediments, compaction of deeply buried strata and recent faulting. Compounding the problem has been the construction of the Aswan High Dam and the consequential loss of sediment delivery to the delta. Agricultural production, which primarily supports the Egyptian population, has been severely hit. Unless remedial measures are taken, it is argued, the sea may encroach into the delta by 30 kilometres in the next hundred years.

The diversion of waters to agriculture and the damming of rivers in the US Pacific Northwest have so interfered with the life cycles of salmon that some species risk becoming endangered. Water flow is the critical parameter that is disturbed. The small fish, the smolts, spend too much time in fresh waters and do not adapt well to the salt waters they seek to enter.

In addition, coastal erosion is increasing as a consequence of other societal activities (Weigel, R. L. 'Need for complete beach and nearshore experiments', Unpubl. ms., 1989). The construction of breakwaters and jetties has accelerated natural processes. Eighty-six per cent of California's shoreline is now eroded and ten per cent has been armoured to protect oceanfront construction (Griggs, G. B. 'California's Coastal Hazards', Unpubl. ms., 1989).

Then there is the loss of natural and semi-natural beaches to landfill, agriculture, transportation (especially the construction of airports), industry and housing, as is the case in the Inland Sea and Osaka Bay regions of Japan (Shapiro, 1989). The length of the coastline suitable for swimming and other recreational activities diminished substantially between 1950 and 1982.

Waterfront construction on the southeastern French Mediterranean coast has resulted in the loss of a significant area of the intralittoral zone where the benthic life is richest (Meinesz *et al.*, 1991). Nice Airport, Toulon-La-Syne and Marseilles ports and yacht harbours, in addition to dikes, landfills and artificial beaches, have combined to destroy nearly ten per cent of the shallow water zone between 0 and 20 metres. As a consequence, the sea grass *Posidonia oceanica*, essential for undersea flora and fauna in thearea, has been to a large extent destroyed. These developments and the loss of the populations are essentially irreversible.

The loss of beaches and the continuing coastal erosion through human activities are well-known problems throughout the world. Scientists can provide options for their mediation through existing information or through the identification of research needed to provide additional data. The costs of minimizing erosion and renourishing the supply of beach sand are great. As man-induced damage continues, the costs become higher with time.

Complementing the loss and alteration of land-forms is the loss and alteration of marine forms – salt marshes, mangroves and coral reefs. These changes are in part a result of economic forces – the profitable use of mangrove areas for shrimp culture and the capture of fish from coral reefs by dynamite or by nets. Tourists contribute to the erosion of these zones through the collection of corals and indigenous organisms. Counteracting these destructive activities are newspaper and magazine articles and television programmes stressing conservation measures.

Extending the coastal zone

The coastal zone can be extended through additions to the land itself or through the construction of artificial islands. The Japanese have been innovative in this area and are proposing extensive additions to their coastline in forthcoming years. Up to the present time they have built seventeen islands, the largest one being 615 ha in area. Many islands are at distances of 500 m offshore and one is 5 km from shore; they have mostly been constructed in water depths of 10 to 20 m (Shimada and Tamura, 1991; Figure I.1).

The Japanese propose to build a string of artificial islands offshore not only to extend coastal shorelines but also to create calmed-water areas. The latter will extend the coastal zone for marine recreation, mariculture, anchorage of commercial and recreational vessels, waste disposal facilities, research, and perhaps wave energy production (Shimada and Tamura, 1991).

The impacts of island construction upon the environment must be continually assessed, especially erosional processes on land and alterations to marine life. The changes in the topography as a consequence of the construction will be site-specific and their effects must be continually under observation.

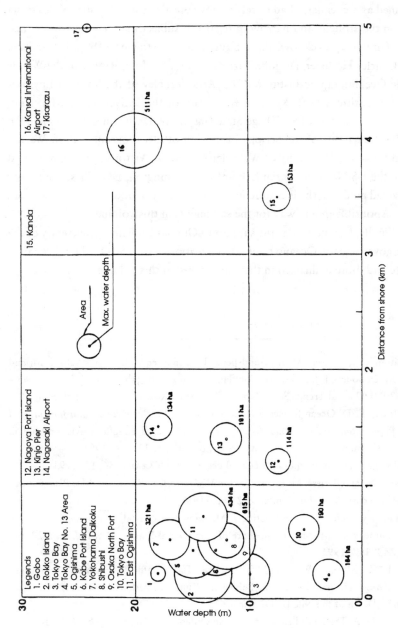

Figure I. 1. Artificial islands in Japan (Shimada and Tamura, 1991)

Acknowledgements

Trained as a chemist, I had to rely on my colleagues in other disciplines to set me on the straight and narrow in regard to subject matter with which I had little familiarity. I acknowledge the guidance given to me by Dr. Judy Capuzzo, Dr. Charles Hollister, Dr. John Farrington and Dr. John Ryther of the Woods Hole Oceanographic Institution; Dr. Arne Jernelev of the Swedish Environmental Institute; Prof. Kenneth R. Tenore of the University of Maryland; Prof. Kathe Bertine of San Diego State University; Dr. Justin Lancaster and Dr. Richard Seymour of the Scripps Institution of Oceanography; Prof. Warren Wooster of the University of Washington; and Dr. Victor Linnenbom, retired from the US Naval Research Laboratory, Washington, DC. These colleagues provided guides to the literature for which I am most grateful. They clearly are not responsible in any way for the statements in this volume.

Finally, I acknowledge the support of Gunnar Kullenberg, Secretary of the Intergovernmental Oceanographic Commission of UNESCO, who is becoming more and more embroiled in the issues posed in this volume.

References

Culliton, T. J., Warren, M. A., Goodspeed, T. R., Remer, D. G., Blackwell, C. M. and McDonough, J. J. 50 years of Population Change along the Nation's Coasts, 1960–2010. Coastal Trends Series No. 2, US NOAA. Rockville, Md. 41 p. (1990).

Goldberg, E. D. Ocean Space: Use and Protection. *In: Resources, Environment, and Population: Present Knowledge and Future Options*, ed. Kingsley Davis and Mikhail S. Bernstam. Oxford University Press, London. pp. 221–34 (1991).

Goldberg, E. D. Competitors for coastal ocean space. *Oceanus* 36, 12 (1993).

Grenon, M. and Batisse, M. *Futures for the Mediterranean Basin. The Blue Plan.* Oxford University Press, London. xix + 279 p. (1989).

Meinesz, A., Lefevre, R. and Astier, J. M. Impact of coastal development along the southeastern Mediterranean shore of Continental France. *Mar. Pol. Bull.* 23, pp. 243–347 (1991).

Ruddle, K., Morgan, W. B. and Pfafflin, J. R. *The Coastal Zone: Man's Response to Change.* Harwood Academic Publishers, Chur, Switzerland. 549 p. (1988).

Science. Death of the Nile Delta? *Science* 250, 1084 (1990).

Shapiro, H. A. The landfilled coast of Japan's Inland Sea. *Ocean Yearbook* 7, eds. E. M. Borgese, N. Ginsburg and J. R. Morgan. University of Chicago Press, Chicago. pp. 294–316 (1989).

Shimada, H., and Tamura, T. Creation of new offshore space: artificial islands and calmed-water areas. Presented to the Second International Symposium on Coastal Ocean Space Utilization, 2–4 April 1991. Long Beach, California, USA (1991)

Vartanov, R. V. USSR coastal zone utilization priorities and concerns of new government policies. Presented at the Second International Symposium on Coastal Ocean Space Utilization, 2–4 April, Long Beach, California, USA (1991).

World Bank. *The Environmental Program for the Mediterranean: Preserving a shared heritage and managing a common resource.* ix + 93 p. Washington, D.C. (1990).

... ...

1. The rising population in the coastal zone

Fifty per cent of the population in the industrialized world lives within one kilometre of a coast. This population will grow at about 1.5 per cent per year during the next decades. The availability of coastal resources, whether on land or on sea, will not be dealt with equitably. Consider the resident of a coastal town who seeks a Sunday at the beach with his family but is forced to return when a place to park the car could not be found. Or in another country, the family would forego such recreation for fear of exposure to enteric viruses and bacteria from domestic waste discharges to the sea.

Introduction

The attraction of the coastal zone as habitat is widespread. The world's coastline is about 440,000 km in total length (Inman and Nordstrom, 1971). Estimates of the percentage of people living near the coast lines of the oceans and large lakes cluster about 50 per cent, although the definition of the coastal zone is both operational and pragmatic. Recent studies in the United States (Culliton et al., 1990) and France (Grenon and Batisse, 1989) have used the smallest political or geographical sub-units for which there are recognizable involvements with marine systems and for which there are appropriate population and economic data.

There can be conflicts among those seeking to exploit the resources of the coastal zone. Thus, it is crucial to be aware of the varied uses of this part of the marine environment, of its economic and social values, and of the need for possible regulatory activities to preserve the resources.

Herein, the renewable resources of the coastal zones and the impacts upon them by growing populations, hoping for a more bountiful life style, will be investigated. The use of the coastal zone for the production of food and chemicals (mariculture), for waste space, for transportation facilities and for tourism and recreation as well as for possible energy production, commercial fishing, and mineral recovery, will be considered. The utilization of these resources puts stresses upon the marine environment, stresses that are not linear with increasing numbers of peoples. Indeed, they may be multiplicative. Perhaps the fragility of the coastal zone may be measured by a stress multiplier, similar to the economic multiplier in social science.

Present and predicted populations in the coastal zones of two areas, the United States and the Mediterranean Basin for which there have been recent scholarly studies, will be examined. Those data provide a stepping stone to understand the conflicts that will arise over competing uses of the coastal zone in the forthcoming half century.

The Mediterranean study

This investigation provides an economic, social and geographic framework, using present understanding, to predict the future developments in the countries of the basin (Grenon and Batisse, 1989). The coastal zone was taken to be composed of administrative territorial units which border the oceans and which form decentralized components of executive authority. These coastal zones, provinces, departments, governorates, etc. possessed the appropriate statistical data. The coastal strip so defined was continuous and had a water depth usually less than 100 m. This zone curiously overlaps the biogeographical one of the extent of olive trees.

The study models the interactions between the environmental components of the Mediterranean Basin and the economic factors such that predictions can be made for the years 2000 and 2050. The environmental components include the soil, the inland waters, the forests, the coast and the sea. The major economic sectors are agriculture, industry, energy, tourism and transport. The rising population will attempt to use the environmental components to the fullest.

Critical to the models are forecasts of future populations. The complexity of world population trends is illustrated by the Mediterranean which is subdivided into three regions of differing growth rates: Region A (Spain, France, Greece, Italy and Yugoslavia); Region B (Algeria, Egypt, Libya, Morocco, Syria and Tunisia); and Region C (Albania, Cyprus, Israel, Lebanon, Malta and Monaco). In the following discussion it should be emphasized that we are dealing with countries, not the coastal zones of countries.

The total population of the Mediterranean Basin will more than double between 1950 and 2025. The populations of the southern and eastern countries (Regions B and C) will rise above the northern countries (Region A) in about 1990 (Fig. 1.1). Most countries are showing declines in gross birth rates and gross death rates and the annual rates of natural population increase will go from slightly under 1.5 per cent in 1980 to slightly under 1 per cent in 2020 (Fig. 1.2). In France, Italy and Spain the birth rates fell in the period of 1974–1985 below the level of replacement (2.1 children per woman). The fertility rate (children per woman) will reach the level of replacement for the whole Mediterranean area in about 2020 (Fig. 1.2).

Perhaps a factor of equal or even greater importance in population change involves immigration (Grenon and Batisse, *op. cit.*). There has been a dramatic reversal in the movements of people in the EEC countries during the second half of the twentieth century. At the beginning of the period about half of the

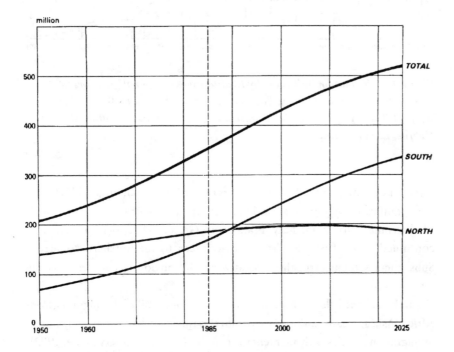

Figure 1.1. Population in the Mediterranean countries: trends 1950–1985 and average scenario 1985–2025. The rate of population growth in the Mediterranean countries as a whole tends to level off as from around 2000. The population of the southern and eastern countries exceeds that of the northern countries as from 1990. (Grenon and Batisse, 1989.)

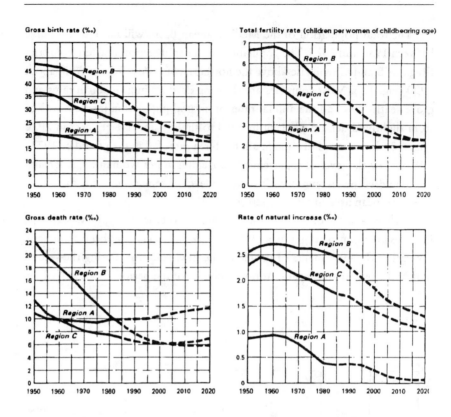

Figure 1.2. Population indicators by Mediterranean regional grouping.
Region A: Spain, France, Italy, Yugoslavia, Greece. Region B: Turkey, Syria,
Egypt, Libya, Tunisia, Algeria, Morocco. Region C: Monaco, Malta, Albania,
Cyprus, Lebanon, Israel.

foreign population in the EEC states was of Mediterranean origin. Now there is a significant migration of nationals from the countries of the southern Mediterranean to Spain, Italy, France and Greece. Thus, one can expect a continued flow of peoples from the southern to the northern countries. Subsequent settlement in the coastal zone will obviously put stress on the resources there.

Italy has been flooded recently by a wave of a million immigrants from Africa, Asia and eastern Europe. Up until this time Italy had remarkably liberal immigration policies with an intent to create a multiracial society (Stille, 1992). The laws were formulated in March of 1990 but at the present time 75 per cent of the Italian citizens favour closing the border to all new immigration. The recently arrived migrants in search of work and prosperity exacerbated an already serious unemployment problem, created a perception of being purveyors of crime, disease and drugs, and, most of all, were very evident by their appearance. Often out of work and without housing, they flooded the beaches of Rimini and Tuscany. The government infrastructure has been unable to cope in an unregulated environment. Clearly a moratorium upon immigration may provide a period to alleviate the situation.

Migration patterns, much like economic or meteorological trends, are difficult to predict. Although controls on migration flows between countries are increasingly being instituted, those who are moving are less inclined to pay attention to the laws than to social and economic opportunities and pressures.

The US study

The population trends for thirty coastal states, including those bordering the Great Lakes, for the years 1960–2010 (predicted) were investigated (Culliton et al., 1990). The country was divided up into five regions: the Northeast, the Gulf of Mexico, the Great Lakes, the Southeast, and the Pacific Region. Four of the five regions have been studied by NOAA in its National Estuarine Inventory Program (NOAA, 1990). The Great Lakes Region was excluded.

Political subdivisions were used to define coastal areas, with the argument that their activities, even though miles inland, can influence the quality of the coastal zone. The 451 coastal counties compare with 1569 non-coastal counties in the studied states. The coastal counties account for 20 per cent of the nation's land area. One hundred and ten million people, almost one-half of the US population, live in the coastal zone today.

During the 50-year period, 1960–2010, it is predicted that the coastal population will grow from 80 million to more than 127 million, an increase of nearly 60 per cent (Table 1.1). The non-coastal states will experience a smaller growth (Fig. 1.3). The northeast and Pacific states today have the largest coastal populations (Fig. 1.4). The state of Florida, which is entirely coastal, will grow from 5 million in 1960 to more than 16 million by 2010, an increase of over 200 per cent. Similar dramatic growths are predicted for California and Texas. Seventeen of the states with the largest predicted population increases are coastal. The five states with the greatest rises in population are California, Texas, Florida, Georgia and Virginia. It is in these states that problems may first become evident in the overuse of the coastal zone resources.

Some parts of the coastal zone will experience decreases in the coming decades. The coastal counties with the greatest population losses are in Alaska and around the Great Lakes (in the study the coasts of the Great Lakes are considered a part of the coastal zone). Due to industrial and agricultural setbacks in states of the Great Lakes, eight of the twenty counties with the highest population declines between 1980 and 1986 were in this area of the United States.

There is quite a difference between the densities of people in coastal and

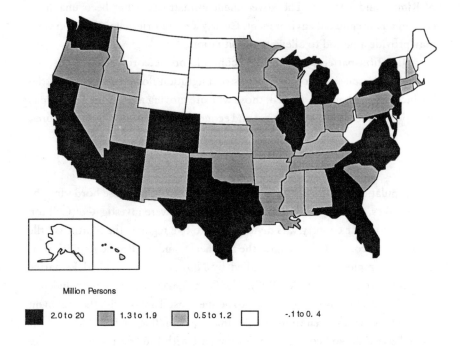

Million Persons

■ 2.0 to 20   1.3 to 1.9   0.5 to 1.2   □ -.1 to 0. 4

Figure 1.3. US population change, 1960–2010
(Culliton et al., 1990)

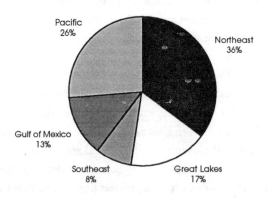

Figure 1.4. Regional distribution of the US coastal population
(Culliton et al., 1990)

Table 1.1. *US coastal and non-coastal population change,*
1960–2010 (Culliton et al., 1990)

Counties	1960	Percent change 1960– 1970	1970	Percent change 1970– 1980	1980	Percent change 1980– 1990	1990	Percent change 1990– 2000	2000	Percent change 2000– 2010	2010
Coastal	80	17	93	9	101	11	112	8	120	6	127
Non-coastal	101	11	112	13	127	9	138	7	148	5	156
Total	181	14	205	11	228	10	249	7	268	6	283

non-coastal zones. Overall in the United States 61 persons on average occupy a square mile of space. In coastal states 100 persons are found per square mile and 248 persons per square mile in coastal counties. The most dense populations of the coastal zone in 1988 were found in the northeast and in the District of Columbia, where the densities are greater than 1000 persons per square mile. In 1988 over 101 counties had population densities of more than 500 persons per square mile. Some counties, which include or surround the cities of New York, San Francisco, Boston and Philadelphia, had populations exceeding 10,000 people per square mile.

Culliton et al. (*op. cit.*) suggest population per shoreline mile as a unit of 'environmental stress'. The following figures were computed from the coastal population of a state by the total shoreline mileage. An average for US coastal states in 1988 is 1177 persons per shoreline mile, with a projected ratio of 1358 in 2010. The coastal states with the highest values, primarily as a consequence of short shorelines and high populations are: Illinois, 91,740; eastern Pennsylvania, 30,871; Indiana, 15,951; and the District of Columbia, 15,049.

Although demographic predictions of this type are imprecise, still they provide guidance as to where to look for future use conflicts. Inevitably, there will be increased demands upon the resources of the coastal zone, be they recreational, food, transportation or waste sites. Growing needs for water, power, facilities for travel and food will exacerbate these problems.

References

Culliton, T. J., Warren, M. A., Goodspeed, T. R., Remer, D. G., Blackwell, C. M. and McDonough, J. J. Fifty Years of Population Change along the Nation's Coast. Second Report of the Coastal Trends Series. Office of Oceanography and Marine Assessment. US National Oceanic and Atmospheric Administration. 41 p. (1990).

Grenon, M. and Batisse, M. *Futures for the Mediterranean Basin. The Blue Plan.* Oxford University Press, London, xix + 279 p. (1989).

Inman, D. L., and Nordstrom, C. E. On the tectonic and morphologic classification of coasts. *J. Geol.* 79, 1 (1971).

NOAA. Estuaries of the United States. Office of Oceanography and Marine Assessment. US National Oceanic and Atmospheric Administration, 79 p. (1990).

Stille, A. No blacks need apply. *Atlantic Monthly* 269 (2), 28–38 (1992).

2. Tourism and recreation

Tourism probably accounts for at least 5 per cent of the world's combined gross national products. It is perhaps its largest industry. The coastal zone is a major attraction drawing both national and international visitors. Nations in the developing world, especially small islands, may have economies dependent upon continuous and increasing tourism. However, the activity is threatened by conflicting demands for coastal ocean space with other pursuits. In addition, there is the continued entry of toxic pathogens and chemicals to coastal waters with potential threats to human health, primarily through the ingestion of seafoods and secondarily through exposure. Worries about an unhealthy quality of the marine environment can have an inhibitory effect upon the advancement of tourist activities.

Introduction

Tourism, both national and international, is placing a higher and higher stress upon the coastal zone. The increased expectations of the world citizenry to travel, coupled with increased leisure time and financial resources, support this human mobility. The coastal zone with its many beach and water activities and ready availability of seafood accommodates a substantial portion of touristic activities.

There is a multitude of recreational activities taking place in coastal areas, some of which require large expanses of beach and water (USDOI, 1981):

1. Beach activities with water contact encompass swimming, wading, surfing, wind- surfing, snorkling, skin-diving and scuba-diving. Non-water contact open-beach activities include hang-gliding, horseback riding, outdoor sports, dune buggy driving, walking, jogging, sunbathing, fishing and shell-fishing and camping.
2. Boating activities involve sailing, scuba-diving and pleasure boating, including water skiing.
3. Sports fishing.

Tourists are defined as temporary visitors spending at least 24 hours in the country visited for purposes of leisure (pleasure, holiday, health, study, religion or sport) and/or business (mission, conference, or family) (World Tourist Organization, which maintains statistical data).

World tourism increased from 160 million to 341 million between 1970 and 1985, an annual growth rate of 4.88 per cent (Grenon and Batisse, 1989) and as a consequence has become one of the largest industries in the world (OECD, 1991). Tourist receipts are rising at a rate greater than general consumer expenditures. In most OECD countries, the tourist revenues continue to rise year after year (Table 2.1).

The needs of coastal zone space to satisfy touristic demands include sites for hotels, for recreational activities on beaches, for transportation facilities (berths for ships, marinas, guided tours, adequate highways, etc.) for restaurants, for casinos, and for aesthetic pleasure.

The Mediterranean Basin countries accounted for 35 per cent of the world tourist market in 1984 (Grenon and Batisse, 1989), the annual growth being 4.48 per cent per year between 1970 and 1986. However, the developing countries in general experienced higher growth rates, the more developed countries lower annual values; above or equal to 10 per cent: Cyprus, Egypt, Greece and Turkey; 5 to 10 per cent: Turkey, Malta, Israel, Morocco and Syria; and 3–4 per cent; France, Spain, Italy, Yugoslavia. Algeria and Libya had no active touristic development.

Tourism may be the world's largest business (Miller and Auyong, 1991). There are some data on the contribution of tourism to national economies, but few on the involvement of the coastal zone, even though it must be high. One quantitative survey was carried out by the OECD (1989) to consider the economies of tourism in its member countries (Table 2.2). The contributions clustered about 5–10 per cent of the gross national product. For many countries of the developing world the contributions must be higher.

The contributions to the total tourist economy from that of the coastal zone has been approached by Grenon and Batisse (1989). They submit that in France, 18 per cent of the domestic tourism and 19 per cent of the international tourism is involved with the Mediterranean coast. For Tunisia and Yugoslavia

Table 2.1. International tourist receipts in millions
of current dollars (OECD, 1991)

	Receipts 1988	Receipts 1989	Percentage 89/88
Austria	10,094.7	9,316.1	-7.7
Belgium-Luxembourg	3,434.7	3,063.5	-10.8
Denmark	2,423.0	2,311.1	-4.6
Finland	984.1	1,013.0	2.9
France	13,784.1	16,500.0	19.7
Germany	8,478.4	8,657.6	2.1
Greece	2,392.6	1,997.7	-16.5
Iceland	107.5	107.6	0.0
Ireland	997.1	1,070.0	7.3
Italy	12,398.5	11,987.4	-3.3
Netherlands	2,872.9	3,019.9	5.1
Norway	1,467.3	1,217.9	-9.5
Portugal	2,425.2	2,587.1	6.7
Spain	16,691.4	16,252.0	-2.6
Sweden	2,346.5	2,543.2	8.4
Switzerland	5,738.1	5,619.2	-2.1
Turkey	2,355.4	2,556.5	8.5
United Kingdom	10,999.8	11,248.4	2.3
Europe	99,991.3	101,178.5	1.2
Canada	4,600.1	5,013.3	9.0
United States	28,935.0	34,432.0	19.0
North America	33,535.1	39,445.3	17.6
Australia	3,295.1	3,369.7	2.3
New Zealand	1,009.9	1,001.0	-0.9
Japan	2,894.2	3,155.6	9.0
Australasia-Japan	7,199.3	7,526.3	4.5
OECD	140,725.7	148,150.1	5.3
Yugoslavia	2,024.2	2,230.4	10.2

*Table 2.2. The contributions of tourism to the economies
of some OECD nations (OECD, 1989)*

United States	6 % of Gross National Product (GNP); US $293 billion. Includes residents and international visitors
Canada	4 % of GNP
United Kingdom	4 % of GNP; greater than 9 billion pounds
Switzerland	6.2 % of Gross Domestic Product (GDP); 16.9 billion Swiss francs
Turkey	3 % of GNP; 2 billion US dollars
Yugoslavia	10 % of foreign exchange earnings
Portugal	9 % of GDP
Norway	3.3 % of total gross product; NKr 36.8 billion
New Zealand	3.9 % of GDP; NZ $2.3 billion
Italy	8.0 % of GDP; 70–75 billion lira
Germany	4.6 % of national income; 96 billion DM
France	390 billion French francs
Finland	40 % of export of goods and services; MK 4.1 billion

the comparable international figures are 80 and 90 per cent respectively. At the present time there are no signs of decline, or to the other extreme, there is no saturation of facilities. Touristic revenues do compensate in many of these countries for the deficits arising from food and fuel imports.

The direct entry of tourists to the coastal zone from the cruise market shows double-digit growth (OECD, 1991). The world cruise fleet is composed of 250 ships with 150,000 berths. The major cruise areas are the Caribbean (80 per cent of the world's market), the Mediterranean (15 per cent) and the US Pacific Coast (Table 2.3).

For small countries, especially those without industrial or agricultural outputs, tourism can be a substantial part of the economy. The Caribbean islands to a large extent support their populations from tourism, which has been steadily rising during the past decade. (CARIB, 1990). In 1987, 5.6 million

*Table 2.3. World cruise population in thousands
(OECD, 1991)*

Cruise area	1984	1985	1986	1987	1988
North America	1,630	1,950	2,340	2,730	3,200
Europe	220	250	200	300	330
Other	150	160	160	170	190
Total	2,000	2,360	2,700	3,200	3,720
Growth rate (%)	–	18.0	14.4	18.5	16.3

cruise passengers came to Caribbean ports, an increase of 12 per cent over the previous year. The contribution of tourism is estimated to be 43 per cent of the GNP of the region (Miller and Auyong, 1991). The percentage contributions of hotel and restaurants to the gross domestic production of some island nations between 1980 and 1987 are but a part of the touristic income but do provide a measure of its economic significance, especially since the data are available. Shop sales, tours and native performances can raise these numbers significantly.

Table 2.4. Percentage contributions from hotels and restaurants to the gross domestic product of various countries of the Caribbean (CARIB, 1990)

Country	1980	1984	1987
Anguilla	25	28	
Antigua and Barbuda	14	15	15
Aruba	26		
British Virgin Islands	30	21	24
Cayman Islands	8	8	
Dominica	1	1	1
Grenada	4	5	7
Montserrat	3	4	4
Netherlands Antilles	4	10	
St. Kitts and Nevis	4	5	12
St. Lucia	6	7	7
St. Vincent and Grenadines	2	2	2
Trinidad and Tobago	0.4	0.4	
Turks and Caicos Islands	18	30	

Table 2.4 shows the contribution from hotels and restaurants to the gross domestic product in countries of the Caribbean, and emphasizes the extremely high involvement of tourism in the economies of some countries (Aruba, Virgin Islands, Anguilla, and Turks and Caicos Islands). However, they are somewhat misleading. For example, Aruba has no industry other than tourism; it imports all of its food; it produces water by distillation of seawater; tourism encompasses its entire economy.

Similarly, the very low values for some of the islands indicate an inducement to the greater development of tourism in the future.

Tourism revenue can compensate for that lost to imports (Grenon and Batisse, 1989). For example, it accounts for 27 per cent in Spain, between 10 and 20 per cent in Cyprus, Malta, Tunisia, Greece, Israel, Morocco and Italy. For Italy, the tourist moneys are equal to one third of the hydrocarbon imports, or 80 per cent of the food deficit.

It may be that one out of 16 persons is employed in activities related to tourism (L. Garrison, cited in Miller and Auyong, 1991). A non-trivial part of the workforce is involved in tourist activities in the Mediterranean (Grenon and Batisse, 1989). This encompasses ten 10 cent in Israel and between 3 and 6 per cent in such countries as Malta, Italy, Spain, Tunisia, the former Yugoslavia and Greece.

These involvements are complemented by the grey or underground economies that do not declare income derived from such activities as the letting of furnished rooms, catering, the building trades and currency exchange.

There are interferences associated with the continuous development of touristic ventures. For example, marine transportation is a substantial part of tourism and yet it can have a serious negative impact through deliberate or accidental discharges from vessels. Beaches soiled by oil or litter do not attract visitors. In the Mediterranean about 2,000 merchant ships are present at any given time, between 250 and 300 of which are tankers (World Bank, 1990). The oil lost from these vessels primarily from discharge of bilge and ballast waters accounts for about 75 per cent of its entry to the Mediterranean; the rest comes from land-based industrial activities and social discharges. About 30 per cent of the oil spilled forms tars that accumulate on the beaches. This insult, coupled with discharges of plastics and other debris from vessels, and the illicit dumping of hazardous materials, challenges the pleasures derived from the coastal zone, a situation of serious consequence to tourism.

The stress on populations of a developing country through the dependence on tourism as a major factor in the economy is well seen in the Caribbean island of Barbados (Bird and Nurse, 1988). The coastal resource in the past has supported small harbours for local and overseas shipping, fishing, some agriculture and small boat construction. These have been challenged and, in some cases, lost to tourism. The west side of the island, with a 92 km coastline, has witnessed a major hotel development over the past 25 years or so, the primary attractions being the natural and artificial coral beaches and the sea. The number of tourists has risen from 40,000 to a quarter of a million per year over the past quarter century. The winter months are especially attractive.

As part of the development of Barbados one part of the shoreline has been beautified by the development of beaches. On the other hand beaches elsewhere have been destroyed and reduced to coral rubble. Pollution threatens the reefs and swimmers alike. Public beach accesses have been minimized through resort construction. Fishing bases have gone. Land prices have sky-rocketed and land purchase is no longer readily available to the native population.

The unaffected part of the island in the northeast contrasts with the touristic area in the zone of the major city Bridgetown on the west and the airport in the southeast. One can still enjoy a relatively unaffected east coast with its somewhat less desirable climate, hopefully a compensation for the local citizens with the contributions to the economy in the tourist zone.

Pathogens

The recreational pursuits in coastal areas can be jeopardized by other profitable activities. Mariculture and the recovery of oil and gas can compete for the same space as that desired by recreational users.

However, of greatest concern are the problems of micro-organisms stemming from domestic waste disposal into marine waters which jeopardize the quality of seafood and recreational activities on beaches both in developing and developed nations. Residents and tourists look to coastal areas as a source of rest and recreation as well as of seafoods, and quite obviously they will be directed away from regions where their health might be endangered. There are economic and social facets to the problem; for countries seeking a more secure financial footing, the loss of tourist revenue in the short term must be balanced against the costs of improved sanitation facilities. For the developed nations, the priorities accorded the recreational amenity must be broached in the political arena.

Two challenges to public health arise from the depositing of pathogens into the coastal zone. First of all, there is the risk through exposure in the waters or on the beaches. Swimmers swallow water; they can take it up through body orifices. However, most information about illnesses through exposure is anecdotal rather than epidemeological. Still there are reports to national and international agencies relating ear, nose and throat disorders, respiratory infections and gastro-intestinal infections to recreational contact with microorganisms of the coastal zone.

The present status of the exposure problem is well described by Godfree *et al.* (1990): '(it)...has received considerable research attention during the last decade with little concrete progress to facilitate the definition of appropriate standards for the management and control of perceived risks'. The following background information is taken from this presentation.

Up until 1972 there were no microbial quality standards for seawaters; all proposed standards were derived from freshwaters. The British had sought relationships between marine bathing and the occurrences of poliomyelitis and enteric fever. Their scientists suggested that waters with median coliform counts of greater than 10,000 per 100 ml might occasionally induce paratyphoid fever. But they also argued that the risks were extremely low. Reasonable guidance came from the argument that there is little risk unless the waters are so polluted with sewage as to be 'aesthetically revolting'. US workers had failed to find any relationship between illnesses of bathers in marine waters and water quality in the early 1970s. The need for refined epidemeological studies was felt in both countries.

In the early 1970s the US EPA initiated a series of investigations to identify relationships between exposures of swimmers on 'barely acceptable beaches' and the occurrence of highly credible gastro-intestinal symptoms (vomiting, diarrhoea, fever, nausea, and stomach ache). The controls were 'relatively unpolluted beaches'. A covariance between the morbidities and exposures was found. An acceptable standard, 'the swimming-associated gastroenteritis rate', was derived as a geometric mean value of 200 faecal coliforms per 100 ml which would result in 19 illnesses per 1000 bathers at marine bathing sites. In addition, not more than 10 per cent of the samples should exceed 400 faecal coliforms per 100 ml. The robustness of these EPA criteria will be assessed in future studies of morbidities associated with swimming in the coastal zone.

In the meantime, the relationships between morbidities and sentinel pathogen levels have been seriously questioned. Critics argue that the protocol has tests which are not reproducible. Illnesses are based upon perception not upon clinical and laboratory analyses.

In 1989/1990 the United Kingdom initiated a series of rigidly controlled tests in which swimmers were examined after exposure to waters of known microbial quality. The subjects could not be asked to bathe in known unacceptable areas; instead they used waters in compliance with present UK standards. This strategy is reasonable since there is an ongoing debate as to whether or not these standards are stringent enough.

Developing and developed countries which still introduce domestic wastes into coastal waters will look forward to future developments to ascertain what levels of treatment will reduce morbidities to acceptable levels in economically rational ways. Perhaps the newly developed protocols will utilize viral sentinels. Some of these pathogens have much longer survival times in marine waters than other micro-organisms.

A far more important threat to public health comes about from the consumption of contaminated (usually raw) shellfish. There is a substantial database associating illnesses and even mortalities with the consumption of seafoods contaminated with toxic viruses and bacteria (Noble, 1990 and Ahmed, 1991 provide up-to-date surveys, emphasizing US problems, from which much of the following discussion is taken).

Most diseases are related to the consumption of bivalves; fish and crabs are less frequently the carriers of the pathogens (Table 2.5). The former group of organisms feed through the filtering of large volumes of water, up to litres per hour, with the removal of suspended particles. In addition to small living plankton, the bivalves also take from the waters bacteria, viruses, and plant toxins produced during bloom periods. The plant toxin problem will be

*Table 2.5. Hazards and risks from seafood consumption
(adapted from Ahmed, 1991)*

	Toxin vector	Impact
Raw bivalves	Viruses, enteric bacteria, *Vibrio* species	Mostly mild gastraoenteritis
Raw or cooked bivalves	PSP, NSP, DSP, ASP toxins* in dinoflagellates	Moderate to severe Mortalities
Finfish	Ciguatoxin in dinoflagellates	Moderate to severe
Processed seafood	(1) *Clostridium perfringens;* (2) *Salmonella;* (3) *Shigella;* (4) *Straphylococcus aureus,* (5) *Vibrio parahemolyticus* (6) Hepatitus A virus (7) *Clostridium botulinum*	Usually mild gastric illnesses. Can be minimized by adequate cooking; temperature control, proper processing and food service

* PSP, paralytic shellfish poisoning; NSP, neurotoxic shellfish poisoning;
DSP, diarrhoetic shellfish poisoning; ASP, amnesic shellfish poisoning.

considered in Chapter 3. The viruses are more important than bacteria in inducing illness. The bivalves which act as disease vectors include clams, scallops, cockles, mussels and oysters.

Pathogenic viruses that bring about human disease enter recreational waters and bivalve habitats primarily through domestic waste disposal. The most important viral agents are the Hepatitis A virus and the Norwalk virus. The latter by far is the more significant. It is responsible for one-half of the occurrences of epidemic non-bacterial gastroenteritis in the United States. In 1982 there were outbreaks involving 103 well-documented cases in New York State alone. Eighty per cent were associated with the eating of raw clams and the rest with eating raw oysters. Insufficient heating can lead to viruses not being killed. Opening of shells does not in itself guarantee adequate treatment, as opposed to the attainment of temperatures of 100 °C.

Another group of diseases is related to the consumption of bacteria such as those responsible for typhoid fever and cholera. The latter pathogen has recently reentered the US scene. No cases were reported between 1911 to 1973 but from 1973 to 1984 31 illnesses were attributed to eating raw seafood, especially oysters.

Tourism in some areas exposes the travellers to naturally occurring seafood-borne diseases like Ciguatera. This affliction is most common in the Caribbean and Pacific islands and can be imported to other areas. It caused about half of all seafood intoxications in 1987–1988 in the US, although mortalities are low. The toxin is presumed to originate in microscopic dinoflagellates

(*Gambierdiscus toxicus*) that grow on tropical reefs. Fish eat the algae and then in turn become toxic. Hundreds of species have been implicated, such as the snapper, goatfish, grouper and barracuda.

The Global Problem: A world-wide review of the health of coastal marine environments carried out by UNEP revealed widespread contamination of seafoods with toxic micro-organisms. The associated morbidities suggest that this is an important marine pollution problem, even though it is only weakly addressed, if ever, at international marine pollution meetings and by authors of text and reference books. The data in Table 2.6, taken from UNEP publications, illustrate the extent of the problem.

These observations from developing countries must be evaluated cautiously. Clearly, there is the potential for disease through exposure to untreated waste waters or through consumption of tainted seafood. On the other hand, in countries that have inadequate husbandry of waste, the case for the association of illness with the marine environment may be weak, for there are other sources of micro-organisms: drinking water, local foods, and human-to-human infection.

The perception of illness from toxic pathogens in coastal waters through the consumption of seafoods or exposure to waters can result in the loss of revenues, especially if there has been a recent well-publicized incident in the country to be visited by potential tourists. Balancing revenues from tourism against sums necessary for the proper management of micro-organisms and toxins can vex environmental managers. Still, positive steps to minimize illnesses from shellfish and fish consumption can be made through educational programmes which emphasize the avoidance of raw shellfish consumption, the appropriate cooking of all sea products and proper processing and serving of the products in local establishments.

Management schemes can take the form of discharge control of wastes or the inspection of the marine products before public sale. Educating the consumers to the dangers of eating raw seafoods is clearly a necessary tactic.

Eutrophication and tourism

Eutrophication in coastal areas can aesthetically insult beaches and adjacent waters through the accumulation of rotting marine plants. This happens in the northern Adriatic where agricultural and domestic wastes from the Po Valley cause the phenomenal growth of algae in the coastal waters adjacent to the tourist areas. The loss in tourist revenue to northern Italy, Croatia and Slovenia is significant, as is the loss in recreational facilities to the local inhabitants of these areas.

Table 2.6. Pathogens in coastal waters

Area	Situation	Reference
Red Sea	Clams with 1000 organisms. Bay of Aden. Untreated sewage discharged to inner waters.	UNEP-1
East Asian Seas*	PSP poisoning leading to mortalities and mor bidities have occurred in Indonesia, Thailand and the Philippines. Records of human disease associated with swimming in polluted waters are lacking. In 1988, 1396 cases of hepatitis were reported of which 591 were confirmed as hepatitis A and 76 as Hepatitis B in Hong Kong. Half of the victims had consumed shellfish before the onset of the disease.	Gomez *et al.*, 1990
Mediterranean	Frequent algal blooms and red tides in coastal waters receiving untreated domestic/industrial wastes - North Adriatic, Izmir Bay, Efesis Bay and the lagoon of Tunis.	MAP, 1989
Southeast Pacific	Hydrofaecal pollution is associated with juvenile diarrhoea.	UNEP-3
South Pacific	Diseases associated with the consumption of sewage contaminated seafood (cholera, typhoid) are increasing in many of the islands. Paralytic shellfish poisoning is growing and it is believed it is related to pollutant levels. Ciguatera remains a major problem with incidences of one to four cases per thousand reported in the Pacific Island Region.	Brodie *et al.*, 1990
South Asia	Gastro-intestinal disease outbreaks resulting from consumption of contaminated seafood in India, Bangladesh and Sri Lanka occur. In the Maldives where seafoods are not eaten, no diseases related to waste disposal have been reported.	Sen-Gupta *et al.*, 1980
West & Central Africa	High risk of infection from consumption of seafoods. No statistical data.	Portman *et al.*, 1989
Red Sea	The coastal areas adjacent to human habitats are contaminated by faecal microbes.	UNEP-1
*Black Sea	Cholera epidemics related to consumption of seafoods from the estuarine areas of the Black Sea of Azov and the Black Sea.	Balkas *et al.*, 1990

* Some deaths reported.

The impacts of tourism

Conflicts in use can also arise from touristic activities themselves. Perhaps the textbook example of recent vintage involves the impact of tributyltin (TBT) compounds used in antifouling paints applied to the bottoms of recreational craft upon maricultured oysters. TBT is the most effective anti-fouling agent ever devised for use in the marine environment. However, these compounds are among the most toxic anthropogenic compounds introduced into marine waters. They have been shown to cause physiological damage to such organisms as the dogwhelk at levels of parts per trillion in the environmental waters, with females developing male characteristics and failing to reproduce.

The first episode took place in Arcachon Bay, France, where 10 per cent of the country's oysters are produced (Goldberg, 1986). In the late 1970s the oysters were found to be producing deformed shells and the oyster spat did not settle. Healthy oysters transplanted to the area suffered 50 per cent mortalities. The diffusion of TBT from marinas to the oyster growing areas was identified as the cause of the problem. In 1982 the French Government banned the use of paints containing TBT on vessels shorter than 25 m. Within several years the oyster production approached normal figures.

Subsequently, other countries, as well as some states in the United States, followed the lead of the French in the regulation of these toxic substances in marine paints. In most cases the legislation was enacted to protect the vitality of all plants and animals which were susceptible to the toxic action of the compounds, as opposed to only that of the commercially-valuable species.

Once the restrictions on the use of TBT in marine paints come about, the imposex problem slowly goes away. For example, on the Northumbrian coast, north of the River Tyne in the United Kingdom, imposex in dogwhelks gradually disappeared between 1986 and 1989 (Evans *et al.*, 1991) after the partial ban on TBT use in 1987. There was a better survivorship of females and an increase in the number of juvenile and adult females, although complete recovery did not occur. Anti-fouling paints without TBT are under development and self-polishing polymers appear an especially attractive alternative (MPB, 1991).

Tourists themselves can contribute to the waste and pollution of the host country (Grenon and Batisse, 1989). The impacts cannot be quantified but in principle may be identified as degrading influences on the quality of the coastal zone: (1) *noise:* primarily from transportation – automobiles, trucks, aeroplanes, ships, the transporting equipment noted above; and (2) *solid and liquid wastes:* the tourists add to those contributed by the residents. The possibility of these wastes affecting public health through the over-taxing of sewer systems or through inadequate disposal systems of pleasure craft must be continuously under assessment.

Littered beaches can be a major deterrent to the continued influx of tourists. In the Mediterranean coastal litter is primarily land-based compared with that of the western European shores where it is marine-based (Gabrielides *et al.*, 1991). This survey covered 13 beaches in Spain, Italy (Sicily), Turkey, Cyprus and Israel between 1988 and 1990. The beaches did not undergo cleaning by local groups. They were sampled once a month and pieces larger than one to two cm were counted. Plastic items made up the most abundant category, followed by wood, metal and glass items. Fishing gear was rather rare. Some beaches were washed clean of litter by high waves during the winter. Litter increased during the summer through the discards of bathers, indicated by the fact that most containers (plastic, metal and glass) had been used for beverages, food and suntan lotion. Items indicative of marine based activities, containers for household detergents and lavatory cleaners, were absent.

Protected marine areas

The establishment of marine parks to protect the ecology of coastal areas can support tourism, offer unique research facilities and maintain an important heritage of our society (Cognetti, 1986; 1990). Competition for space with incompatible industrial and other productive activities demands active intervention on the part of national and international bodies. The marine parks can take many forms: fishing reserves, natural marine reserves, study areas and diving areas with cultural and scientific aims.

The development of marine park areas has proved especially promising in the Mediterranean where the Council of Europe has been supportive (Cognetti, *op. cit.*). France has the most extensive programmes with 16 areas designated for special care. Spain does not distinguish land parks from marine parks and often the former incorporate the latter. Greece established three marine parks primarily for the protection of monk seals and marine turtles. Other northern and eastern Mediterranean countries with marine reserves include Israel and Italy. There are a few marine reserves in Egypt; Tunisia set up a marine park on the Island of Zembra where the rare monk seal is still found.

Innovation in the development of marine parks that allows the public to come into contact with marine plants and animals without the use of diving gear may be economically reasonable. Structures to allow entry to the coastal environment on such a basis are conceivable.

References

Ahmed, F. E. *Seafood Safety.* National Academy Press, Washington, D.C. xv + 432 p. (1991).

Balkas, T., Dechev, G., Mihnea, R., Serbanescu, O. and Unluata, U. State of the Marine Environment in the Black Sea Region. UNEP Regional Seas Reports and Studies No. 124. iii + 41 p. (1990).

Bird, J. B. and Nurse, L. The coasts of Barbados – An economic resource under stress. *In: The Coastal Zone: Man's Response to Change,* ed. K. Ruddle, W. B. Morgan and J. R. Pfafflin. Harwood Academic Publishers, Chur Switzerland. pp. 197–211 (1988).

Brodie, J. E., Arnould, C., Eldredge, L., Hammond, L., Holthus, P., Mobray, D. and Tortell, P. State of the Marine Environment in the South Pacific Region. UNEP Regional Seas Reports and Studies No. 127, iv + 59 p. (1990).

CARIB. *Caribbean Tourism. Statistical Report.* 1989 Edition. Caribbean Tourism Organization. Marine Gardens, Christ Church, Barbados, West Indies, 195 p. (1990).

Cognetti, G. Perspectives for protected marine areas in the Mediterranean. *Mar. Poll. Bull.* 17, 185–6 (1986).

Cognetti, G. Conservation of Marine Environments in the Mediterranean. *Mar. Poll. Bull.* 21, 185–6 (1986).

Evans, S. M., Hutton, A., Randall, M. A. and Samosir, A. M. Recovery in populations of dogwhelks *Nucella lapillus* (L.) suffering from imposex. *Mar. Poll. Bull.* 22, 331–3 (1991).

Gabrielides, G. P., Golik, A., Loizides, L., Marino, M. G., Bingel, F. and Torregrossa, M. V. Man-made garbage pollution of the Mediterranean coastline. *Mar. Poll. Bull.* 23, 437–41 (1991).

Godfree, A., Jones, F. and Kay, D. Recreational Water Quality. The management of environmental health risks associated with sewage discharges. *Mar. Poll. Bull.* 21, 414–22 (1990).

Goldberg, E. D. TBT: An environmental dilemna. *Environment* 28, 17–21 (1986).

Gomez, E. D., Deocadiz, E., Hungspreugs, M., Joathy, A. A., Jee, K. K., Soegiarto, A. and Wu, R. S. S. The State of the Marine Environment in the East Asian Seas Region. UNEP Regional Seas Reports and Studies No. 126, iii + 63 p. (1990).

Grenon, M., and Batisse, M. *Futures for the Mediterranean Basin. The Blue Plan.* Oxford University Press. xviii + 279 p. (1989).

MAP. State of the Mediterranean Marine Environment. MAP Technical Report Series No. 28. UNEP. Athens. 225 p. (1989)

Miller, M. L. and Auyong, L. Coastal Zone Tourism Marine Policy. March, pp. 75–99 (1991).

MPB. TBT-free anti-fouling developments. *Mar. Poll. Bull.* 22, 427 (1991).

Noble, R. C. Death on the half-shell: The health hazards of eating shellfish. *Persp. Biol. Med.* 33, 313–22 (1990).

OECD. *Tourism Policy and International Tourism*. Organization for Economic Cooperation and Development. Paris. 217 p. (1989).

OECD. *Tourism Policy and International Tourism*. Organization for Economic Cooperation and Development Plans. 196 p.

Portmann, J. E., Biney, A. C., Ibe, C. and Zabi, S. State of the marine environment in the West and Central African region. UNEP Regional Seas Reports and Studies No. 108. iv + 34 p. (1989).

Sen Gupta, R., Ali, M., Bhuiyan, A. L., Hossain, M. M., Sivalingham, P. M., Subasinghe, S. and Tirmizi, N. M. State of the Marine Environment in the South Asian Seas Region. No. 123. iii + 42 p. (1990).

UNEP-1. State of the Marine Environment in the Red Sea Region. Geneva (1987) Draft.

UNEP-3. State of the Marine Environment in the South East Pacific Region. Geneva (1987) Draft.

UNEP-8. State of the Marine Environment in the Caribbean Region. Geneva (1987) Draft.

US DOI. U.S. Department of the Interior. Inventory and Evaluation of California Coastal Recreation and Aesthetic Resources. POCS Technical Paper No. 81 (1981).

World Bank. *The Environmental Program for the Mediterranean: Preserving a shared heritage and managing a common resource*. ix + 93 p. Washington, D.C. (1990).

3. The role of the oceans in waste management

The role of the oceans in waste management today is subdued if not on hold. The effective petitioning of environmental groups, coupled with a lack of foresight and imagination by regulatory agencies, inhibits attempts to alter the present situation. As a consequence, the waste capacity of the oceans is greatly under-utilized. Still, the rising costs of land disposal with more and more evidence that terrestrial resources like subterranean waters, soil and air are being threatened, force an examination of this stance. Many scientists and engineers are advocates of some sea disposal of some wastes in some places, but this message has not been effectively relayed to the general public. In spite of a modest anticipation for a greater use of the oceans for waste disposal in the future, it is recognized that some important marine pollution problems today relate to the improper disposal of domestic and industrial wastes to the sea.

Introduction

In the last decades of the twentieth century, there has been little enthusiasm for the use of the oceans as a waste receptacle. Both national and international policies were dedicated to land and air disposal strategies for societal discards. The seas were considered sacrosanct and were not to be soiled.

This mood evolved from the recognition by scientists in the early 1950s that the composition of the oceans could be changed by human activity. The initial motivating force was the developing nuclear energy industry. The concern was the uncontrolled release of artificial radionuclides to the atmosphere and to the oceans, with a consequential challenge to public health through environmental exposures and the consumption of contaminated foods. Subsequently sovereign nations and international groups developed guidelines for maximum acceptable levels of artificial radionuclides in the marine environment. Releases from nuclear energy facilities, the principal sources, were regulated on the basis of the protection of highly exposed individuals.

Simultaneously, there was a growing concern that societal wastes were entering the marine environment and altering ecosystems. This was first pointed out by Cottam and Higgins (1946), two US Fish and Wildlife Service scientists, in regard to the impact of the pesticide DDT upon non-target organisms.

These problems were dramatically elaborated upon by Rachel Carson (1962) in her book *Silent Spring*. Pressures from the natural and social science communities led the US Environmental Protection Agency in 1972 to strongly restrict the use of DDT as an agricultural biocide. Later, additional chlorinated hydrocarbon pesticides were to be banned by the United States and other developed countries.

These events, stimulated by the activities of scientists, gave birth and sustenance to environmental organizations which took on the roles of the protectors of the environment. Through their dedication to improving our surroundings, they were most attractive to socially conscious citizens. The groups became powerful in sponsoring legislation in many countries. Their zealousness often directed them to formulate their own concepts about environmental problems, concepts often in conflict with conventional scientific wisdom.

Also, in the late 1970s and 1980s, governmental agencies came into prominence whose charge was to regulate activities that might threaten the quality of the environment. Much like the environmental organizations, they sometimes operated outside the realm of the prevailing concepts of scholars. At times driven by technophobia and anti-scholarship these groups have alienated many in the scientific community.

At the same time critical assessments by scientists and engineers of ocean waste disposal practices have, in general, been positive. For example, a 1989 review of sewage sludge disposals in twelve areas of the United Kingdom (MAFF, 1989) indicates that there was no real evidence that the disposal of sewage sludge has an impact on the marine environment at any site except that in the Clyde estuary. This site is the least dispersive of the sites used for sewage sludge disposal and, even here, the scale of impact is limited.

Or the results of the US Crystal Mountain Workshop (Goldberg, 1979):

'...the waste capacity of US coastal waters is not now fully used. The largest US ocean dumpsite (Dumpsite 106, about 196 km southeast of the entrance of New York Harbor off the New Jersey coast) is not used to its total assimilative capacity. Here the endpoint is defined as an unacceptable disturbance to the community of organisms.'

In the early 1970s some most significant regulatory developments were taking place at both national and international levels. Conventions were formulated to limit or perhaps totally stop ocean disposal of wastes. The importance of these conventions rests upon the conviction that the oceans can be seriously damaged by societal activities. The enforcement of the international provisions rests with individual states who have jurisdiction over their territorial waters and the operation of their flag ships.

The Oslo Convention for the Prevention of Marine Pollution by Dumping from Ships and Aircraft, was adopted on 15 February 1972 by the Scandinavian states who were prompted by the proposed disposal of 650 tons of chlorinated hydrocarbons in the north part of the North Sea (Side, 1986). This action provided the stepping stone to other agreements. The Helsinki Convention on the Protection of the Marine Environment of the Baltic Sea area was adopted in 1974 and the Barcelona Convention for the Protection of the Mediterranean against pollution in 1976. The London Dumping Convention, which was first initialed by 57 countries in 1972 (*Mar. Poll.*, 1972) now has 91 signatories. The London Dumping Convention addresses global concerns; the others being directed to more specific regional problems (Norton, 1981).

In general, the provisions of the conventions are similar except that the Helsinki Convention prohibits all dumping in the Baltic with the exception of dredge spoils, an action which requires a permit from an appropriate agency in the disposing nation.

These Conventions respond to scientific understanding of how ocean resources can be jeopardized by the entry of toxic substances or benign materials that threaten living organisms. It is not clear as to the goals of the members. Some participate to prevent all ocean disposal where alternate land options are available; the others seek specific regulations as to what materials can or cannot be discarded in the oceans, utilizing such philosophies as 'assimilative capacity' (see following).

In the London Dumping Convention regulated substances are classified into two annexes following the initial model of the Oslo Convention: Annex 1 for which ocean disposal is banned; and Annex 2 for substances that require special care. Annex 1 substances include organohalogen compounds, mercury and mercury compounds, cadmium and cadmium compounds; persistent plastics and other persistent synthetic materials; crude oil, fuel oil, heavy diesel oils and lubricating oils, high-level radioactive wastes, materials produced for biological or chemical warfare and benign substances that cause marine organisms to be unpalatable or that endanger the health of organisms including human beings.

Annex 2 encompasses the following chemicals: arsenic, lead, copper, zinc, cyanides, fluorides and their compounds and pesticides and their by-products not covered in Annex 1: large volumes of acids or alkalies, especially those that might contain beryllium, chromium, nickel and vanadium; materials that might sink to the sea bottom and interfere with fishing or navigation; and low-level radioactivity.

The London Dumping Convention does not define the extent of the coastal states jurisdiction. Further, it does not restrict a nation from adding additional materials to Annex 1 or Annex 2 (Bruce, 1986).

The Conventions are modified as new information is acquired. For example, consultative meetings are held annually at the International Maritime Organization (IMO) in London during which the Convention can be revised. In 1985, the organosilicon compounds were proposed for removal by the scientific group on dumping from Annex 2 (*Mar. Poll.*, 1986) on the basis of their non-toxic nature. Previously, the Oslo Convention had removed these compounds from their list of prohibited substances. However, the London Dumping Convention disregarded this advice, to the frustration of the scientists (Peet, 1991).

In 1987 the dumping of persistent plastics at sea became a part of Annex 1 (Wolfe, 1987). Ingestion of plastic debris had been shown to jeopardize the well-being of seabirds, those most affected being shearwaters and albatrosses. The adults feed the young by regurgitation. Young birds unable to regurgitate can experience blockages of the gastro-intestinal track and internal lesions and can die following the consumption of plastic debris passed on by their parents. Entanglement of marine mammals in abandoned fishing gear or plastic container holders can also result in mortalities. Thus, the London Dumping Convention prohibits discharge of persistent plastics and persistent materials such as netting and lines which may float or remain in suspension in such a manner as to interfere materially with fishing, navigation and other legitimate usages of the sea.

Finally, the IMO has brought together a Convention for the Prevention of Marine Pollution from Ships (MARPOL) which has been adopted by 57 countries representing over 85 per cent of the world's merchant fleet. The Convention prohibits the disposal of plastics from ships and strongly regulates the ways other rubbish such as food wastes, papers, metal cans, etc. can be dropped into the oceans from ships. A complete disposal ban also exists for dunnage (lining and packaging materials that float). These provisions have been extended to platforms and drilling rigs.

Certain marine areas especially vulnerable to pollution because they are landlocked or environmentally sensitive, have been designated by MARPOL as 'Special Areas'; these include the North, Mediterranean, Bering, Red and

Baltic Seas. All dumping is prohibited with the exception of food wastes which can be discarded twelve miles off land.

By the end of the 1980s the countries of the developed world were bewildered by the intricacies of the problems in domestic and industrial waste disposal. Waste disposal issues of all kinds were capturing attention in the communications media. In the United States, the citizenry of some US states were belligerently opposing the transport to their area of wastes generated in others. For example, New Jersey and New York send 55 per cent and 11 per cent respectively of their trash outside their own boundaries (NYT, 1990). These two states were responsible for about 50 per cent of interstate waste transport and they are the largest movers. Indiana, for example, estimates that 20 to 30 per cent of its solid wastes comes from out of the State, yet it has only six to eight years of landfill capacity left. On a national basis, it is estimated that 8 per cent of domestic waste is involved in interstate transport. The exporting states find it uneconomic or extremely difficult to open up new landfills or construct incinerators. Yet they face legislation from some states prohibiting the importation of wastes or increasing the costs of disposal of out-of-state wastes.

Garbage scows were seen on world television in the 1980s traversing the oceans and seeking a port in which to discharge their cargoes. Ships loaded with toxic wastes from one country were refused entry to a second country. However, the economics of waste disposal led some financially distressed developing nations to import discards for disposal. For example, in February 1988 Guinea agreed to take 15 million tons of pharmaceutical wastes from the United States and Europe for $600 million (Vir, 1989). On the other hand, Congo turned down a contract to receive a million tons of solvent, paint and pesticide sludge and chemical waste from these areas. A treaty to restrict the international movement of toxic wastes was formulated in Basel, Switzerland in March 1989 under the auspices of the United Nations. The treaty does not ban the shipments of hazardous wastes; it does prohibit the entry of exported materials into a country without that government's written consent.

Thus, the waste husbandry situation at the beginning of the last decade of the twentieth century could be described in the following way. Both international and national legislation had formulated guidelines for the disposition of hazardous and benign wastes. The developed countries were running out of terrestrial waste disposal sites. The oceans had ceased to be an acceptable option. Incineration, a waste disposal alternative, had met public opposition through fears of the atmospheric dissemination of toxic substances such as dioxins, mercury and cadmium. The Third-World countries were developing a resistance to the importation of wastes from the industrialized nations.

Types of wastes

The nature and production rate of a waste should, in principle, determine its ultimate fate. For convenience, it is appropriate to characterize wastes in a general way as domestic, agricultural and industrial. A sub-division of all three encompasses hazardous wastes. Among them are the discards containing artificially-produced radioactive nuclides which in recent times have spearheaded our concern about marine pollution. Data from the United States will be used to illustrate our descriptions of waste types.

The United States, with a population around 250 million, generates about 1280 million metric tons of wastes annually, the materials falling into the categories given in Table 3.1. With the exception of the industrial wastes, most of these materials are benign with respect to creating health hazards.

Table 3.1. Waste materials generated annually by the United States (EPA, 1990)

	Million metric tons	Per cent of total
Municipal solid waste	180	14.1
Sewage sludge	300	23.4
Dredge materials	400	31.3
Industrial waste, wet and solid	400	31.3

Industrial wastes

In the United States the amount of solid waste produced by manufacturers has been around 200 million short tons per year, i.e. about a ton per person per year. It may be decreasing as concerted attempts are made to reduce waste production and to recycle. Chemical and primary metal industries are the largest generators. In the former, a dominant source is the phosphate fertilizer industry.

About 10 per cent of the wastes can be categorized as toxic. They arise primarily from the smelting and refining of primary metals, the electroplating of metals and the production of organic chemicals.

The classic case of an industrial discharge disaster in the marine environment involved the wastes from a Japanese plastics manufacturer, Chisso Chemical. Unwanted residues from its production process were discarded into the semi-enclosed basin, Minimata Bay. The materials included manganese, organic chemicals and mercury. Although a problem first came to light in the early 1950s, it took over a decade to identify the offending chemical. Mercury was found to have accumulated in fish and shellfish as methylmercury, a potent neurological poison. It first affected cats consuming waste seafoods, which exhibited unusual and neurotic movements. The morbidity became known as the 'dancing cat disease'. Subsequently, fishermen and their families were struck by the toxin and severe illness and death ensued (Goldberg, 1976).

The Minimata Bay episode received unusual notoriety, especially as some of the victims appeared at the 1972 Stockholm Environmental Conference. The tragedy is often cited as a terrifying example of the toxicity of waste metals which somehow or other enter the marine environment and subsequently the human food chain. Fortunately, this mercury poisoning episode, along with those concerning tributyltin and copper, are almost unique cases of serious metal pollution in the marine environment (Goldberg, 1992).

The successful operation of a US industrial waste disposal site has been halted by legislative action at the national level recently. Dumpsite 106, 196 km southeast of the entrance of New York Harbour and 185 km east of Cape May, New Jersey, just beyond the edge of the continental shelf, has water depths between 1800 and 2700 m. Since 1972 it has received discards from a variety of industries and some domestic wastes. Wastes have been brought to the area by barge or tanker, usually in around 4000 cubic metre lots. The wastes are fed to the waters and sink gravitationally at rates not exceeding 70 to 120 cubic metres as regulated by the Environmental Protection Agency. No serious impacts upon surface marine organisms were observed (Capuzzo and Lancaster, 1985).

The fate of materials disposed at this deep ocean site has been studied by Grassle (1990) whose models denied conventional wisdom that domestic sewage sludges would be dispersed in the water column and would not reach the bottom. Samples were collected by a submersible from depressions that might trap the sludge particles. On the basis of trace metal concentrations, bacterial spores of *Clostridium perfringens*, a human sewage indicator, and the stable isotope ratios found in animals living in the sediments, it became clear that measurable amounts of sludge are reaching the bottom. Such knowledge can be the springboard for studies on how the disposed materials may affect the communities of deep-sea organisms. Ocean dumping officially ceased at Dumpsite 106 on 30 June 1992 by federal mandate.

Domestic wastes

These discards encompass the solids and liquids that arise from day-to-day living in homes. Their management has been quite a perplexing problem to the political systems of developed nations. At the village or city level, searches continue for land disposal sites that are becoming more and more scarce with each succeeding year. Yet the production of solid wastes continues to rise; in 1980 it was about 180 million tons per year or about 3/4 ton per person per year in the United States (EPA, 1990). Because of the increasing distances between sites of generation and sites of disposal, the costs of moving the wastes become higher and higher. Pleas are continually made to recycle or to reduce the domestic wastes and these actions are becoming somewhat effective. Recent technological assessments of the problem do not consider the ocean option at all because of prohibitory federal regulations. The only solid wastes that have been disposed of at sea, besides dredged material, are sewage sludges. Garbage (paper, trash, etc.) has not been dumped since the 1960s. The only sewage sludge now dumped is from communities in and about northern New Jersey and New York City. A little over 7 million tons was dumped in 1987. These sludges are now dumped at the 106 mile site (L. Swanson, personal communication).

Since over 50 per cent of most domestic wastes (paper, food and yard wastes, leather, textiles, etc.) can be incinerated, reduction by burning continues to be attractive. In spite of successful incineration practices in many cities of the world, it is opposed by many environmental groups who are concerned with toxic emissions. Furthermore, the ash which often constitutes 25 per cent of the bulk waste, must be disposed of in some way or other.

The direct discharge of domestic waste, along with some industrial and agricultural wastes, into the coastal ocean may be abetting some of the most serious marine pollution problems on the global scale. These include the growing eutrophication of the waters and the increased frequency of red tides and plankton blooms as a consequence of the introduction of the plant nutrients phosphate and nitrates which foster primary plant production (Smayda, 1989, 1990). Entry of these biostimulants can be made through sewer pipes, dumping, waste runoff or rivers, as well as through the atmosphere. For example, in the North Sea near Helgoland, inorganic N and P levels doubled and tripled respectively between 1962 and 1984 as a consequence of Elbe River discharges. In Tolo Harbour, Hong Kong, N and P levels doubled between 1976 and 1985. As a consequence, there has been an increase in phytoplankton production and an alteration of species composition (NOAA, 1979). The siliceous diatoms, which are the food base for filter-feeding fishes and zooplankton and which largely support the coastal commercial fisheries, are being displaced by the dinoflagellates and other non-siliceous algae, as the Si/N and Si/P ratios have decreased. These latter organisms are a poor food substitute for the diatoms. Further alterations of the community structure can take place, including an increase in production and range of macrophytes (sea grasses and attached algae).

Plankton blooms (including the red tides) encompass events in which high concentrations of unicellular phytoplanktonic organisms come about (IOC, 1987). The factors responsible are as yet ill-defined and perhaps may be multiple and different for each event. They may be biological, physical and/or chemical. In such episodes, the plant growth rates must exceed the losses due to sinking, lysis and grazing. Higher levels of nutrients than found during non-bloom periods are assumed to contribute to the process.

The effects of the blooms include discoloration of the water, foam production, the production of organisms bearing toxic substances, changes in community structure and increased production of organic matter resulting in high levels of consumption of oxygen as it sinks to the bottom.

The numbers of organisms involved in toxin production are rather small. There are three primary types of poisoning: PSP, paralytic shellfish poisoning; DSP, diarrhoeic shellfish poisoning; and NSP, neurotoxic shellfish poisoning. Only PSP results in human death in severe cases. DSP causes diarrhoea, while NSP ingestion can result in respiratory distress and skin irritation.

There are continued reports of human mortalities from the ingestion of bloom organisms on a worldwide basis. Increased frequencies and intensities of toxic organisms are reported for Australian waters, especially those species inducing PSP. In 1980 two human deaths occurred and there have been others since then, but none before (Hallegraeff, 1987). In 1986 15 shellfish farms had to be closed due to high levels of toxin and subsequent closures of five farms had to be imposed in 1987.

An IOC Workshop (IOC, 1987) surveying plankton blooms and red tides throughout the world concluded that the phenomena are global and appear to be spreading geographically and increasing in both extent and frequency. Although the primary concerns involve human health through the ingestion of toxic substances in the red tide organisms which were taken up by filter feeders, the impact upon shellfish and finfish resources, both natural and farmed, has serious economic consequences. For example, red tides of *Chattonella antiqua* have caused massive kills of farmed fish, mostly yellowtail, in the Seto Inland Sea of Japan (IOC, 1987). A similar event occurred in Antifer, France (near Le Havre), where the entire stock of a fish farm perished after a red tide dominated by *Exuviaelola* producing a PSP toxin (Jenkenson, 1987). Clearly, the increasing intensities and frequencies of red tides can bring about untold economic losses by mariculturers. Perhaps one necessary expense in the future will be the formation of monitoring systems to assist in the prediction of red tides and the development of preventative measures for farmers.

Waste discharges from one country can markedly influence the environmental resources of another. This has been seen quite dramatically in the northern Adriatic where domestic, agricultural and industrial wastes are introduced through rivers causing extensive plant growth. Tremendous plankton blooms have occurred and the impact upon tourism has been stunning, with beaches abandoned during the height of the season in Adriatic coastal areas in both Italy and the former Yugoslavia.

Because of the enhanced productivity there is an increased flux of organic matter to the sediments. Further, with large discharges to the coastal waters of industrial and domestic wastes and with deforestation and land-use changes, there has been a significant entry of anthropogenic organic carbon. Anoxic conditions are developing over larger areas and there may occur changes in the structure of the benthos.

Biomass increases, anoxia and alterations of community structure have been observed worldwide in coastal waters and in estuaries (NOAA, 1979). Chesapeake Bay, the New York Bight, the southern and northern California coasts, the Baltic Sea, Kaneohe Bay, Hawaii, the Adriatic Sea, Oslo Fjord, Omura Bay, Japan, and Tokyo Bay, Japan, are but a few of the zones subjected to these anthropogenic inductions of rising marine plant productivity and to increased organic carbon fluxes from the continents.

There are several long-term studies to illustrate these trends towards anoxia. The annual minimum oxygen concentrations in the bottom waters of fourteen Swedish coastal zones were measured from the early 1950s and 1960s to 1984. In twelve of these stations there was a declining trend (Rosenberg, 1990; Fig. 3.1). Rosenberg attributes these changes to large-scale eutrophication and takes them to be warning signals of potential resource loss unless the inputs of nutrients from domestic wastes and agriculture are significantly reduced. There have been significant reductions in the extent of benthic fauna, most probably as the result of increased periods of anoxia.

Finally, there are serious problems arising from the entry of enteric microorganisms with domestic wastes causing morbidities and mortalities to exposed individuals, especially through the consumption of tainted seafoods. This situation occurs both in the developed and developing nations, yet its seriousness is far greater in the latter.

In spite of these difficulties the coastal ocean can be effectively used in accommodating domestic waste discharges without unacceptable impacts upon public health and recreation. By the appropriate siting of the discharge area and with suitable pre-treatment of the wastes, the coastal oceans can accommodate some of these discards without loss of resources, be they recreation or foods from the sea.

On a global basis most domestic sewage enters the oceans without any treatment. A small fraction undergoes chemical, physical or biological processing. *Primary treatment* involves the removal of the solid phases with densities higher than water, the sinkables, and those with densities less than water, the floatables. Such a treatment can remove a substantial amount of the

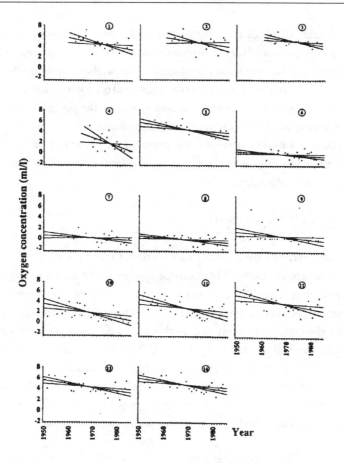

Figure 3.1. Temporal trends in annual minimum bottom oxygen concentrations at Swedish coastal stations. The regression line is shown together with 95 per cent significance level for the slope of that line. (Rosenberg, 1990).

suspended solids; in San Diego, California, for example, 60 per cent of the suspended solids are taken out. A refinement, *advanced primary treatment*, involves another step in which solid phases are added to or are formed in the discharged waters. Settling agents, such as iron chloride which hydrolyses to ferric hydroxides and synthetic polymer coagulants, are introduced into the settling tanks. This process is intended to remove 70 per cent of the remaining suspended solids. During the initial operation of the plant, the suspended solid contents of the sewage waters were reduced from 120 parts per million to 65 parts per million by the additional treatment. The untreated sewage waters contain 243 parts per million of suspended solids.

Secondary treatment involves the microbial oxidation of the organic phases through the addition of bacteria. Again, a substantial reduction in the organic load is sought, although the treatment does increase the amount of sludge produced. San Diego's advanced primary treatment produces around 117 tons of dry matter per day. Secondary treatment could double that figure. Since the sludge must be disposed of and since ocean disposal is no longer legally possible in the United States, the courses of action to handle the sludge include land-fill, incineration and preparation of soil amendments.

Tertiary treatment involves the removal of plant nutrients such as phosphates and nitrates which can otherwise overstimulate plant production and lead to eutrophication.

Dredge spoils

The greatest entry of solid wastes to US coastal marine waters comes from dredge spoils (NAS, 1990). These can be benign with sources in unpolluted sediments; they can also contain toxic materials including petroleum hydrocarbons, pesticides, among others. The disposal sites are distributed along US coasts somewhat uniformly and discharge usually takes place within three miles of the coast. With increasing dredging in harbours there is a tendency to dispose of the wastes, particularly contaminated dredged materials, further from shore. About one-sixth of the dredged materials are dumped outside of the three mile zone (NAS, 1990). Dredge spoils are expected to increase if deep-water ports and further harbour development come about.

Hazardous wastes

The oceans have been successfully used to accept some hazardous wastes and have been proposed as receptacles for others. The term 'hazardous waste' encompasses materials which, if disposed, can jeopardize in any way the viability of living organisms. The production of hazardous wastes throughout the world is startling. The United States generates about one ton per capita annually, most of it coming from industries such as chemical plants, petroleum refineries and manufacturers. There is a more terrifying situation globally. A recent article (Cons. Ex., 1988) states 'in many underdeveloped countries, no facilities exist to handle hazardous waste – whether the waste comes from US multinationals or domestic firms ... some (hazardous waste) generating plants are located in countries without even sewage treatment facilities'.

A notorious example of the disposition of extremely hazardous materials involved military weaponry. The disposal of approximately 67 tons of toxic nerve agents in about 5000 m of water about 400 km east of Cape Kennedy was carried out successfully in August 1970 (Linnenbom, 1971). These highly toxic weapons consisted of 12,500 rockets, some projectiles and a land mine.

They were packaged in steel-encased vaults, which, after the addition of the weapons, were filled with concrete.

The vaults were transferred from depots in Kentucky and Alabama and loaded upon an obsolete World War II Liberty ship at Sunny Point, North Carolina. The vessel was towed to the dump-site where scuttling took place. The ship did not break up upon hitting the bottom and there was no evidence that the marine biota were subsequently affected by any leakages of toxic agents. The discarded nerve gas, isopropylmethylphosphono-fluoridate (GB), rapidly decomposes in water with an estimated half-life of 30 minutes (Epstein, 1970).

Today there may be preferable techniques for the disposal of this type of military weaponry (freezing the projectiles, cutting them up into smaller pieces and incinerating the toxic materials). However, this was a successful husbandry of a very toxic waste, and an interdisciplinary assessment by scholars today still might favour the ocean disposal of the nerve gas by one strategy or another.

Radioactive wastes constitute another group of materials that have posed great problems regarding adequate disposal and storage. The high-level wastes are characterized by heat, radiation and longevity which all contribute to the difficulty of disposal. The fine-grained clays of the deep sea-floor have been proposed as a site in which these very toxic materials might be placed such that any exposure to them by living organisms over periods of thousands of millennia might be minimized (Hollister *et al.*, 1981). The areas of such deposits cover about 20 per cent of the earth's surface.

The important characteristics of the clays are their vertical and lateral uniformity, their low permeability, high cation retention capacity and potential for self-healing, if disturbed. The sediments, called abyssal red clays, have an average particle size of several micrometres with extremely low rates of accumulation, of the order of millimetres per thousand years. The goal of ocean disposal is to isolate the materials for a million or so years, and this requires a stable platform, as demonstrated by past records. Thus penetration of the wastes to depths of several metres places them in sediments which have accumulated over the past several million years.

If the disposal site is chosen away from plate boundaries (i.e. sites of active geologic activity), the sediments will have a low probability of being affected by earthquakes, volcanic activity or other physical disturbances. Furthermore, if the site is far from steep or rugged topographies, the deposits will not be subject to slumping or erosion by deep-sea currents.

It is proposed to place the radioactive wastes, in a chemically stable form, in stainless steel canisters filled with concrete. These containers would then be introduced into the sediments either gravitationally or by an explosive-boosting system which would be activated when the wastes were just above the sediment/ water interface (Fig. 3.2).

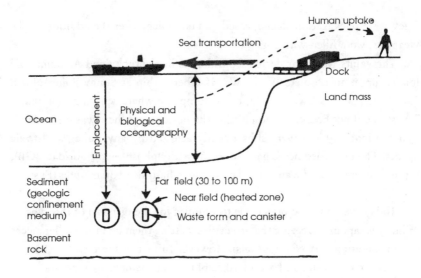

Figure 3.2. Schematic showing range of considerations in examining the feasibility of subseabed waste disposal. It is necessary to characterize the geological barrier and consider the results of leakage or accidental failure to emplace the canister within deepsea sediments. One must be able to trace the migration of escaped radionuclides from the canister site within and through the sediments, water column, and ecosystem in order to evaluate the potential environmental impact of subseabed nuclear waste disposal (not to scale). (Hollister et al., 1981).

Impediments to a possible return of any radionuclides to the waters, organisms or sediments have been engineered into the waste disposal tactics. The barriers are the combined result of (1) the solid form of the wastes, (2) the concrete imbedment, (3) the stainless steel casing of the canisters, and (4) the sediments in which the canisters are embedded. Further, the overlying water column provides a barrier which can retain and dilute any particles that free themselves from the container and can inhibit their entry into the human food chain.

One property of seawater, its salt content, provides a rather subtle advantage for ocean disposal of high-level radioactive wastes. The leaching of man-made silicate glasses, used to solidify the toxic materials, is smaller by two orders of magnitude in seawater as compared to fresh waters (Barkatt *et al.*, 1989). Investigations on the nature of the glass surfaces after exposure indicate that there is a magnesium-rich layer formed on the seawater-exposed materials. This apparently provides protection against attack and subsequent release of contained radionuclides.

Comparison of leach rates with naturally-occurring glasses of similar composition, the tektites, again confirms the lower values in seawater as compared to fresh waters. These tektites have been in place in some marine sediments for periods of around 100,000 years and have experienced only modest corrosion. Barkatt *et al. (op. cit.)* point out that present models of leaching based upon the solubilities of amorphous silica are probably overly conservative. They should be substituted by models where the solubility of magnesium silicates provides the limiting parameter. In laboratory studies of up to 400 days, leach rates in both fresh and seawaters decreased with time. Indeed, corrosion by Pacific ocean seawaters showed negative leach rates, i.e. the uptake of solids upon the glass surfaces, possibly magnesium silicates. In a way these surface coatings form an additional barrier to the entry of radioactive wastes to the ocean environment.

Economic and social considerations will weigh heavily in the assessment of ocean disposal. Two further points are made by Hollister *et al. (op. cit.).* They argue the plan does not conflict with the London Dumping Convention, which prohibits the dumping of high-level wastes or spent fuel *into waters* of the oceans. These authors argue that the high level wastes will be placed *beneath* the seabed. On the other hand, environmental groups take the position that ocean disposal of radioactive wastes is banned by the London Convention (Mar. Poll., 1988).

The preliminary costs estimates of Hollister *et al. (op. cit.)* are comparable to those associated with using a mined repository on land. Thus, the feasibility of ocean disposal of radioactive wastes merits continued discussion in the face of the overwhelming social and economic problems associated with the identification of acceptable terrestrial sites.

There is even conflict between the scientific community and special interest groups in the disposal of low-level radioactive wastes in the deep ocean. Since the early 1960s a number of European countries have used a dumpsite in the Northeast Atlantic abyssal plane with an average depth of 4400 metres for low and intermediate level wastes. The discharges have been coordinated by the Nuclear Energy Agency of the Organization for Economic Cooperation and Development (OECD). In August 1982 the environmental organization Greenpeace interfered with the dumping of British and Swiss low-level waste. In 1983 the British ceased disposal as a consequence of a ban by members of the British Seaman's Union against any involvement with ships that carry such wastes (Mar. Poll., 1985). An initial review by the United Kingdom Commission argued the best practicable disposal option should be sought through a comparison of land and sea options. The group recognized the dilemma of choosing any specific strategy, especially by those whose immediate surroundings might be affected.

In 1987 the Oslo Commission adopted a recommendation to prohibit the building of new or extending existing nuclear reprocessing facilities unless there be no radioactive pollution of the surrounding waters, i.e. zero discharge (Mar. Poll., 1987).

The disposal of low-level radioactive wastes from nuclear facilities into the sea became a matter of serious public as well as scientific discussion following a television programme in 1983 in which an alleged increase in childhood leukaemia near the Sellafield Nuclear Facilities in the United Kingdom was related to the entry of artificially-produced radionuclides into the coastal waters of the Irish Sea. A commission was formed to inquire into the problem and was headed by Sir Douglas Black, a distinguished legal scholar (Black, 1984).

The Commission concluded that the hypothesis can be neither categorically dismissed nor readily proven. Mortalities from childhood cancer, particularly from those other than leukaemia, appeared to be near the national average of the United Kingdom but the possibility of local pockets of high incidence could not be excluded. The Commission pinpointed some difficulties in relating measured environmental levels of artificial radioactivities to actual exposures. Population exposures are determined in part through measurements of radionuclides in various parts of the environment. There are perhaps unidentified sites of concentration which act as a path back to human society. In addition, unplanned discharges, not detected by the monitoring programmes, could have delivered a significant dose via an unsuspected route. Still, using models with most conservative assumptions, the Commission found no evidence of a general risk to children or adults living near the nuclear facilities compared with that of their near neighbours.

The Report had critics both among the lay public and within the scientific community. Shortly after its issuance in 1984 there were a series of articles in the science magazine *Nature* and in the popular press contesting the conclusion of the Black Commission (see, for example, Pomiankowski, 1984). Sophisticated statistical analyses of the data, only understandable with difficulty, if at all, by the lay public, formed the bases for the disagreement. Both the report and its critics call for further research on the possible health consequences of the discharges.

However, the Black Commission Report, suggesting that there is no demonstrable relationship between the discharges and the incidence of childhood cancer, will not overcome the momentum to greatly decrease the disposal of radioactive wastes into the sea. Present intents of the British Government are to markedly reduce marine discharges over the next decade.

Finally, the oceans do offer places away from human habitation for the incineration of hazardous materials. As the amounts of burnable toxic wastes (often chlorinated organics including the polychlorinated biphenyls and other discards from chemical industries) increase, the available land incineration plants become more and more overloaded. Yet the effective campaigns of environmental groups, coupled with the lack of adequate demonstrations of the capabilities of incineration ships, have all but shut off any possibility of continued use of the air disposal option in the near future.

The largest US disposal firm, Waste Management, Inc., for instance, has abandoned its goal to incinerate such toxic materials as dioxins and polychlorinated biphenyls at sea. It is the only company with incineration vessels in the United States. The United Kingdom announced its intention to gradually reduce incineration to less than 63 per cent of its 1988 level by 1991 (Mar. Poll., 1988). The countries of the London Dumping Convention in October 1988 decided to phase out all marine burning with a goal of a total cessation by 31 December 1994 (Kasoulides, 1988). An explicit concern is that incineration practices will be exported to other parts of the world.

The techniques for ocean incineration for the destruction of hazardous organic wastes were developed in Europe several decades ago (Redford *et al.*, 1988). In the United States, the EPA first considered an ocean incineration strategy in the mid 1970s. Four series of burns were carried out, three in the Gulf of Mexico and one in the South Pacific Ocean near Johnson Atoll. They involved the incineration of organo-chlorine wastes and the herbicide Agent Orange. Following these incinerations, special permits were sought in the United States to burn PCB and DDT wastes. The EPA indicated that there was a lack of an adequate body of knowledge to assess potential health and environmental effects. In February 1989, EPA abandoned all involvement with ocean incineration.

There have been few studies on the emission from the combustion of toxic substances at sea. The guidelines for acceptable concentrations of toxins in the emissions are yet to be spelled out, although for safety reasons destructions of 99.9999 per cent may be necessary. The composition and quantity of toxic materials in real burns and their subsequent dissemination about the environment are yet to be made. Criteria for cleaning the vessels after the burns are crucial. Until such detailed studies are carried out, potential effects upon human health and upon marine organisms are not predictable. The fate of marine incineration throughout the world is at best in limbo and perhaps doomed for the near future. Scientists and engineers who objectively consider the comparative advantages of marine versus land incineration may eventually direct political administrations to the ocean option.

Monitoring schemes

In order to ascertain whether or not the levels of wastes introduced into ocean waters, whether deliberate or unintentional, exceed acceptable values, several schemes have been developed whose aims are to protect public health and the communities of organisms. Two such are: 'The Critical Pathways Approach' (Preston, 1975) of the United Kingdom primarily for the protection of public health and the 'Assimilative Capacity Approach' of the United States (Goldberg, 1979) which essentially extends this concept to the protection of ecosystems.

In the former tactic, each scheme is formulated quantitatively to arrive at a relationship between the rate of introduction of a toxin and the consequential dose to humans. The receiving capacity of the environment is thus based upon insuring that no single individual receives an unacceptable amount of radiation either in food or through exposure.

The technique requires an estimate of the environmental concentrations in the receiving waters based upon source compositions and chemical and physical processes (Fig. 3.3). Following entry to the water mass, the toxin can distribute itself among the solution, living matter and particulates. These quantities can be estimated using existing partition coefficients and concentration factors. The rates of intake of the toxins can then be arrived at using data from environmental surveys which determine the amounts and types of food eaten (i.e. the specific rate of intake) or life styles which expose individuals externally. The maximum safe input rate can then be compared with that based upon International Commission of Radiological Protection (ICRP) standards and the authorized input rate.

After the provisional calculations have been made and the discharges have been initiated, there must be a continuous post-operational waste disposal assessment (Fig. 3.4). Here the effluent analyses and a monitoring of critical materials lead to values of exposure. If they exceed the maximum safe input rate, revisions of authorized inputs can be made.

The United Kingdom has used the critical pathway approach to control the discharges of liquid radioactive waste into the Irish Sea for the past several decades. Details of this activity are published annually by the Ministry of Agriculture, Fisheries and Food, Directorate of Fisheries Research (see, for example, Hunt, 1988, and MAFF, 1990). The goal is to protect public health. The monitoring results are provided in terms of radiation exposures of the public. Judgements are based upon the recommendations of the ICRP. The highest exposed individuals, either through food consumption or the absorption of external radiation, are sought. Thus, 'habits surveys' of exposed populations are made near nuclear establishments. Such data are combined with the results of monitoring to evaluate the risks to the critical groups.

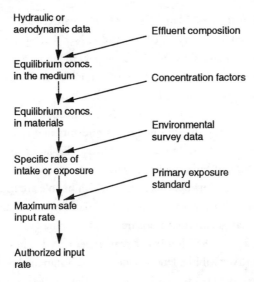

Figure 3.3. Diagram of provisional waste disposal assessment

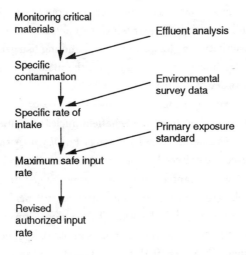

Figure 3.4. Diagram of post-operational waste disposal assessment.

The scheme utilizes the ICRP-recommended principle of a dose limit of 1 mSv/year with a subsidiary limit of 5 mSv/year provided the lifetime average does not exceed 1 mSv/year. The important contributors to radiation exposure are radiocaesium and the transuranic elements. The entry of the latter nuclides will decrease substantially with the operation of an actinide removal plant at the Sellafield facility as from 1992.

Fishermen and their families constituted the critical group in the United Kingdom on the basis of fish and shellfish consumption. Here, the total beta activity, as well as the Cs-134 and Cs-137 levels, were crucial. The most exposed persons consumed 36.5 kg/year of fish and 6.6 kg/year of shellfish. Plaice and cod are the most eaten fish; winkles encompass the important shellfish vector. The critical populations, living near two nuclear facilities, had estimated exposures of 0.19 mSv/year in 1990 (MAFF, 1990).

The external exposure pathway is a consequence of the uptake of radionuclides upon the fine-grained muds and silts in estuaries and harbours as opposed to that of sands on the beaches. The latter are generally poor absorbers of artificial radionuclides. Various coastal areas are monitored for radiation levels. The time periods during which people are in a high exposure area are critical. Those who occupy houseboats in high-radiation zones are subject to the greatest external exposure. Those who had the highest occupancy of houseboats, about 2850 hours per year, experienced exposures of 0.24 mSv in 1987 on the River Ribble. Due to a decreased occupancy on the boats and a declining radioactivity from Sellafield in the sediments between 1987 and 1989, the level fell to 0.17 mSv (MAFF, 1990). Additional exposure through the consumption of seafoods containing radioactivity were considered negligible.

A second pathway that affects another component of the population is through the handling of fishing gear which can entrain particles of sediment containing radioactivity. The longest times of handling fish gear per year were of the order of 500 hours. Using this figure, the maximum exposure would have been of the order of 0.1 mSv.

The classic case using the Critical Pathways approach involved the release of the radionuclide Ru-106 from the Sellafield nuclear facilities into the Irish Sea. The isotope was accumulated by the alga *Porphyra*. A small population in South Wales used the seaweed as an ingredient in a dish called 'laverbread'. The pathway is now dormant as the consumers no longer receive the seaweed from the Sellafield area. However, monitoring is still performed. Recently published information suggests that the effective dose equivalent, that is the percentage of the ICRP recommended limit, is about 0.1 per cent for the most exposed consumers in South Wales. The laverbread story illustrates the approach. The potential culprit is first identified, the critical population is found, and finally the extent of exposure is monitored to ensure that there is minimal risk.

In the Assimilative Capacity scheme, the amounts or fluxes of foreign materials that could be contained or received within a body of seawater without producing a predetermined, unacceptable impact are sought (NOAA, 1979). These values, essentially determined by a titration of the polluting materials with the water body, become evident at an endpoint.

In this scheme it is necessary to identify the exposed organisms whose metabolic functioning can be endangered by the pollutant. For example, the

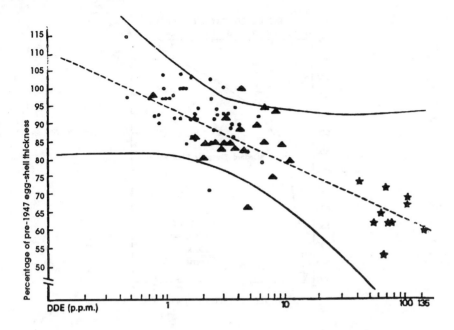

Figure 3.5. The relationship between eggshell thinning and DDE in eighty brown pelican eggs. Solid lines represent 95 per cent confidence limits (Blus et al., 1972). ●, *Eggs from Florida pelicans;* ▲ *, eggs from South Carolina pelicans;* ★ *, eggs from California pelicans.*

impact of DDT and its degradation products such as DDE, as well as other halogenated hydrocarbon pesticides upon fish-eating birds, can provide such an endpoint through the compositions of the associated environmental waters. The ingestion of these organohalides results in eggshell thinning, the eggs become easily subject to breakage through the activities of the birds themselves, and in consequence population declines occur through reproductive failure (Blus *et al.*, 1972). The relationship between eggshell thinning and DDE content in eggs (Fig. 3.5) indicates that DDE and other halogenated hydrocarbon pesticide entries to a marine area should be curtailed, if possible, before the DDE levels in the eggs exceed 1 ppm.

Dissolved gaseous oxygen concentrations have been proposed as an endpoint to limit the entry to the marine environment of compounds with a high biological oxygen demand (Jackson, 1982). He argues that animals cannot live at oxygen concentrations of 4 micromolar or less. Thus sewage sludges, for example, may be introduced to coastal waters as long as this criterion is respected. It is especially attractive since regulation is based on one rather easily measured quantity. Clearly, deviations from the endpoint of less than 4 micromolar oxygen in the waters may occur near the ocean input. The times and areas of acceptable deviations must be stated.

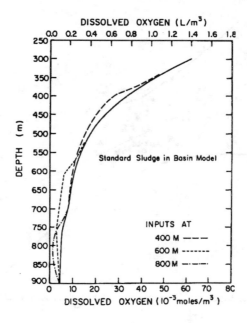

Figure 3.6. Dissolved oxygen concentration in Santa Monica-San Pedro Basin for standard conditions, only oxygen reaction with sludge particles. Sludge inputs are to 400, 600 and 800 m. The solid line represents present no-discharge condition. (Jackson, 1982).

A model was constructed using accepted parameters on mixing processes in the San Pedro-Santa Barbara Basins of Southern California. The disposal of sewage sludge at 800 m appeared to have crucial impacts on the oxygen concentration: the sludge brought the ambient levels of oxygen below 4 micromolar. Shallower disposal, say at 400 m, would not (Fig. 3.6). Thus, easily measured dissolved oxygen gas can flag an unacceptable alteration to the environment.

For many pollutants the monitoring of coastal waters can be effectively carried out through the use of sentinel organisms whose body burdens provide a measure of environmental concentrations. Often, pollutant levels that can bring about disturbances to ecosystems are so low that analyses require quite large and difficult-to-handle amounts of water, and complicated extraction procedures. The Mussel Watch approach (Goldberg, 1975) uses bivalves, usually mussels or oysters, to amass the pollutants, and has been effectively used in many countries (Farrington et al., 1983). The rationale for this approach makes use of the following characteristics of the molluscs:

1. They are cosmopolitan.
2. They are sedentary and integrate pollutant levels at a given site.

3. They concentrate many pollutants over seawater by factors of hundreds to thousands, thus reducing difficulties of analysis. Pollutants that have been successfully measured by this technique include metals, chlorinated hydrocarbons, petroleum hydrocarbons, and some artificially-produced radionuclides.

4. They measure the biological availability of pollutants.

5. They have low metabolic rates for the destruction of some hydrocarbons.

6. They have often stable populations that can be sampled without jeopardizing the vitality of the communities.

7. They survive under conditions that often reduce or eliminate other species.

8. They can be transplanted and maintained in various parts of the marine environment.

9. The biological half-lives of many pollutants in the soft tissues are of the order of months. Thus their body burdens average out exposure levels over such time periods.

The use of sentinels has identified serious pollution problems. For example, the body burdens of polychlorinated hydrocarbons (PCBs) in mussels living in New Bedford Bay, Massachusetts, were at least an order of magnitude higher than those of organisms living in adjacent areas. This anomaly resulted from the discharge of these chemicals from manufacturing plants producing electrical components. The PCB levels in some commercial fish and shellfish were at such high levels that harvesting was prohibited.

Multi-media assessments of waste disposal problems

Scientists and engineers have successfully compared the relative advantages of either land or sea waste disposal for particular substances and for particular sites. It is important to realize that such evaluations can be done objectively. For example, a group of 55 social and natural scientists applied a variety of criteria to ascertain the most reasonable solutions to problems of industrial and domestic waste disposal (NAS, 1984).

Environmentally, biological effects provided the focus of concern. It was recognized that a single index of impact would be most reasonable for political decision makers; it appeared that no such parameter exists nor can one be devised. A matrix of land, freshwater and marine environments with associated ecosystem responses to contaminants was prepared (Table 3.2). Semi-quantitative estimates of potential impacts were made to provide a guide for judgement.

The significant effect to be avoided is species extinction, most critical in streams, wetlands and estuaries. Habitat loss through waste disposal is closely

Table 3.2. Comparison of ecosystem responses to waste imput (NAS, 1985)

Type of environment	Species extinction	Habitat loss	Elevated nutrients	Recoverability	Containment	Remedial action	Uncertainty	Visibility	Pathogen routes to society	Toxicant routes to society
Land										
Disturbed lands*	1	0	1	0	1	0	1	5	5	5
Remnants*	0	5	1	1	1	1	1	5	5	5
Temperature forest	1	1	1	2	1	1	1	3	2	2
Temperature grassland	1	1	1	1	1	1	1	3	3	3
Pasture	0	0	0	1	2	1	1	5	5	5
Agricultural land	0	1	0	2	2	1	1	5	5	5
Arid land	3	2	1	3	1	3	2	2	1	1
Arctic land	0	1	1	5	1	5	4	1	1	1
Freshwater										
Lake	1	5	5	3	5	4	2	5	4	4
Stream	5	5	3	2	5	4	3	3	5	5
Wetland	5	5	5	3	5	5	4	2	3	3
Groundwater	3	1	5	5	5	5	5	0	5	5
Marine										
Wetlands (US East Coast)	1	4	3	3	5	5	3	5	5	5
Wetlands (US West Coast)	5	5	3	3	5	5	2	5	5	5
Estuaries	5	5	3	3	5	5	2	5	5	5
Coastal areas	1	3	1	1	5	5	3	1	3	4
Open ocean	1	1	0	5	5	5	5	0	1	1

Notes:

Species extinction: 5 = greatest concern

Habitat loss. Loss of a significant portion of a habitat type: 5 = greatest concern.

Elevated nutrients: 5 = highest probability of change to ecosystem.

Recoverability. Ability of system to repair itsel after input ceases:
    5 = slowest recovery, decades to centuries; 1= rapid recovery, years.

Containment. Ability of unmodified system to restrict spread of inputs:
    5 = greatest difficulty.

Remedial action. Ease with which we can repair damage to ecosystem:
    5 = greatest difficulty.

Visibility: 5 = most visible.

Pathogen routes to society: 5 = highest probability of reaching society.

Toxicant routes to society: 5 = highest probability of reaching society.

ª Disturbed lands. Land modified by human activities.

ᵇ Remnants. Isolated natural spots within developed or otherwise highly modified areas.

related to the species extinction problem. The increases in nutrient levels which can lead to eutrophication are most serious in estuarine, freshwater and marine wetlands, as well as various terrestrial waters.

The ability of a water body to regain a normal community structure following a large waste discharge episode is most difficult for Arctic lands, open ocean and ground waters, domains where there can be long residence times for pollutants, centuries to millennia. The study also looked at the abilities of waters and lands to contain the pollutants. The waters were uniformly less able to restrict the spread of inputs than the many parts of the solid earth. Finally, the return of toxicants and pathogens to society were in general more easily made via aqueous systems compared with those of land.

Proceeding from these general concepts, two specific disposal problems were considered: municipal sewage sludge and industrial acid wastes from titanium dioxide production. The latter involved options of (1) ocean disposal, or (2) acid neutralization of the wastes with limestone followed by the disposal of the resultant iron sludge to land and the effluents to a stream. The assessment of the alternatives required data about potential impacts upon human health, property and ecosystems, as well as aesthetics, recreation, and concerns about noise and odours. Institutional considerations involved community attitudes, services, economy and safety. Matrices to consider these factors in the two options were prepared (Tables 3.3 and 3.4) and weighing factors were proposed to provide the relative importance of impacts. Clearly, the entries into these tables have a subjective component. But what is important is that a consensus was reached by the involved scientists and engineers to obtain a preliminary assessment of the relative suitability of either option.

The neutralization and land disposal option for the industrial wastes, for example, has a slight effect on air quality as a consequence of the increased emissions of truck engine exhaust gases and particulates. This had a high relative importance but a small impact. Since no irreversible effects were anticipated, the long-term impact was given a value of zero. On the other hand, there is the possibility of long-term effects on groundwaters through the mobilization of the soluble sludge components. The impact factors for human health and welfare and the biota were given a value of one.

The participants at the workshop considered that the land impact would be the greatest, especially as it relates to aesthetics and recreation both in the short and long terms. A high rating of four was assigned to the impact.

Among the institutional considerations, the community attitudes were considered higher in the short term than in the long term. Community services would be affected by the 700,000 truck miles travelled per year through road maintenance and traffic control. The interaction with the economy of the community would be both positive and negative. The creation of employment

Table 3.3. Impact assessment matrix for
neutralization and land disposal alternative

Medium and areas of concern	Relative importance Scale 1–3	Impacts (–5 to +5) Short term Mag.[a]	EEP[b]	Long term Mag.	EEF
A. Environmental considerations					
1. AIR					
a. Human:					
health	3	1	3	0	0
welfare					
(e.g. aesthetics, colour, noise)	2	0	0	0	0
b. Biota	2	0	0	0	0
c. Property	1	0	0	0	0
2. SURFACE WATER					
a. Human:					
health	3	0	0	0	0
welfare	2	0	0	0	0
b. Biota	2	1	2	0	0
c. Property	1	0	0	0	0
3. GROUNDWATER					
a. Human:					
health	3	0	0	1	3
welfare	1	0	0	1	1
b. Biota	1	0	0	1	1
c. Property	1	0	0	0	0
4. LAND					
a. Human:					
health	3	0	0	0	0
welfare	2	4	8	4	8
b. Biota	1	1	1	0	0
c. Property	1	1	1	1	1
5. OCEAN					
a. Human:					
health	3	0	0	0	0
welfare	2	0	0	0	0
b. Biota (benthos, plankton, fish)	2	0	0	0	0
c. Property	1	0	0	0	0
TOTALS			17		14
B. Institutional considerations					
Effects on community					
a. Attitudes	2	4	8	2	4
b. Services	1	2	2	2	2
c. Economy	2	1	2	2	4
d. Safety	3	2	6	2	6
TOTALS			18		16

[a] Mag.: Magnitude of impact on each environmental and institutional resource considered is estimated on a scale of –5 to +5 with negative numbers indicating beneficial impacts (–5 = greatest beneficial impact) and positive numbers denoting harmful impacts (+5 = greatest harmful impact).
[b] EEF: Environmental evaluation factor = (relative importance of environmental variable) x (magnitude of impact).

Table 3.4. Impact assessment matrix for
the ocean disposal alternative

Medium and areas of concern	Relative importance Scale 1–3	Impacts (–5 to +5) Short term Mag.[a]	Short term EEP[b]	Long term Mag.	Long term EEF
A. Environmental considerations					
1. AIR					
a. Human:					
health	3	0	0	0	0
welfare					
(e.g. aesthetics, colour, noise)	2	0	0	0	0
b. Biota	2	0	0	0	0
c. Property	1	0	0	0	0
2. SURFACE WATER					
a. Human:					
health	3	0	0	0	0
welfare	2	0	0	0	0
b. Biota	2	0	0	0	0
c. Property	1	0	0	0	0
3. GROUNDWATER					
a. Human:					
health	3	0	0	0	0
welfare	1	0	0	0	0
b. Biota	1	0	0	0	0
c. Property	1	0	0	0	0
4. LAND					
a. Human:					
health	3	0	0	0	0
welfare	2	0	0	0	0
b. Biota	1	0	0	0	0
c. Property	1	0	0	0	0
5. OCEAN					
a. Human:					
health	3	0	0	0	0
welfare	2	1	2	0	0
b. Biota (benthos, plankton, fish)	2	1	2	0	0
c. Property	1	0	0	0	0
TOTALS			4		0
B. Institutional considerations					
Effects on community					
a. Attitudes	2	4	8	4	8
b. Services	1	0	0	0	0
c. Economy	2	0	0	0	0
d. Safety	3	1	3	1	3
TOTALS			11		11

[a] Mag.: Magnitude of impact on each environmental and institutional resource considered is estiamted on a scale of –5 to +5 with negative numbers indicating beneficial impacts (–5 = greatest beneficial impact) and positive numbers denoting harmful impacts (+5 = greatest harmful impact).
[b] EEF: Environmental evaluation factor = (relative importance of environmental variable) x (magnitude of impact).

at the neutralization plant and disposal operations is positive. On the other hand, property values in the vicinity of these activities would decrease. Maintaining the traffic routes would impact negatively upon the economy. A net result of plus one was proposed. The problem of public safety was considered seriously and given an impact value of two both in the short and long terms. This option would have no effect upon the oceans.

Similar calculations were made for ocean disposal, with the more serious consideration given to effects upon the biota. Ocean disposal would not effect the quality of air, surface water or land and consequently would not impact upon the integrity of ecosystems or public health. The impacts upon the biota were assumed to be localized in the discharge area and to operate only within a short time after discharge. In addition, the effect on human welfare was perceived to be of short duration only and to effect aesthetics and recreational uses of the water. Public safety was given a rating of one on the probability of a collision with bridge structures and of the involvement of the discharging vessels in other shipping accidents. The participants accepted that public attitudes were strongly unfavourable to ocean disposal and that this mood would last over the short and long terms.

The environmental and economic factors favoured ocean discharge whereas the institutional parameters were less inclined toward this alternative. The capital expenditure for ocean disposal was estimated to be about $25,000,000; for land disposal, approximately $48,000,000.

In the case of sewage sludge disposal, public perceptions, regulatory considerations, available technology, environmental risks and economics did not bias a conclusion toward either option. But what is important in this study is that ocean disposal was at least as attractive as land disposal to an inter-disciplinary group of scholars.

Sludge disposal has been especially bothersome to many north European countries. The United Kingdom and Ireland are the only two nations still carrying out disposal into the North and Irish Seas, UK dumpings amounting to 10 million wet tons per year (Mar. Poll., 1989a). These two countries disagree with their neighbours over the impacts of sludge disposal in these areas. Concerns initially centred on the development of anoxia in the sediments of the disposal area and in the increase in the numbers of diseased fish (MAFF, 1989).

Following several years of monitoring sewage sludge disposal sites, the marine environment appeared healthy. The only major effect identified at several sites was the presence of litter attributed to the discharges, which was aesthetically unacceptable (MAFF, 1991a and 1991b). The problems arise when floatables and sewage sludge debris (large detrital materials including plastics, condoms and tampons) enter the discharge area. They can be removed by screening of the sludges. They were marked effects on the benthos at one site (Garroch Head) which did not have effective dispersion. Still, there were no unacceptable effects outside the mixing zone. Furthermore, the fish at this sludge discharge site, as well as all others, had a quality quite acceptable for human consumption). Nevertheless, the United Kingdom does intend to phase out sewage sludge disposal to the ocean by 1998 (MAFF, 1991*b*).

The continuing loss of acceptable land sites for sludge disposal, coupled with these concerns about marine discharges, has, however, led some to consider disposing of sludges in the deep sea. A UK entrepreneur (Davies, 1989) has proposed a deep sea disposal option with especially designed ships for the purpose. Alternatively, a recent UK assessment concluded that the incineration of the sludges would be the economical disposal strategy.

An unusual land/sea assessment of a waste disposal problem involves old nuclear submarines. The US Navy possessed in 1984 about 120 vessels of which the great majority were expected to be taken out of service in the next two or three decades (Navy, 1984). Before disposal the nuclear fuel is taken from the vessel, a process which removes the fissionable material and the fission products. However, there remains some induced radioactivity within the reactor compartment of the submarine: radionuclides produced by neutrons which travelled through the fuel casing and were captured in the metal structures of the reactor unit, forming such species as Fe-55. This structural radioactivity within the metal may be released through dissolution, such as through corrosion.

Three different strategies were considered for the disposition of the vessels:

1. Burial of the submarine reactor compartment with its induced radioactivity at an existing waste disposal site such as the federal plants at Hanford, Washington, or the Savannah River plant in North Carolina. The reactor compartment would be cut free from the vessel. All openings would be welded shut. The non-radioactive remainder would be sunk at sea or cut up for sale as scrap metal. The reactor compartment would be loaded onto a large barge and towed to a river landing near either of the two burial sites. The radiation outside of the compartment would be well below regulatory limits. The time for corrosion to occur in the inner part of the compartment is estimated to be one hundred years. It was calculated that even if 100 reactor components were buried at the same site, the radiation received per person near the site would be well below the average background level of 100 millirem per year, perhaps of the order of 0.006 millirem per year. Even if the person lived and farmed right at the site, whole body radiation of about 13 millirems per year would be received.

2. Place the entire submarine on the bottom of the ocean in deep water. The criteria for ocean disposal include the identification of sites: free of seafood harvesting; free of social, industrial, and maricultural activities; and at

least within 200 miles of the coast, the zone of economic control. These criteria place the disposal sites in areas of deep water beyond the continental shelf. The two Atlantic sites are situated east of Cape Hatteras, North Carolina; the Pacific counterparts are west of Cape Mendocino, California. The water depths are around 2.5–3 miles. The submarines would be towed to the disposal site and sent to the bottom in a controlled flooding operation. The 'worst effects' scenario considered sinking 100 vessels at the same site. Assuming an individual consumed all of his seafood recovered from the disposal site, his or her annual exposure would be 0.0002 millirem, or 2 millionths of normal background exposure. Finally, retrieval of the submarines is possible.

3. Maintain the submarine in protective storage at a ship facility. This is a delaying tactic. The submarine would deteriorate at the disposal site and action under 1 or 2 above would be in order for the future.

The Navy's evaluation of the three options was based upon resource utilization, impacts upon ecosystems, public health, occupational safety and economics. Permanent disposal on land would require about 10 acres or 0.02 square miles for 100 vessels. On the other hand, ocean disposal for the same number of vessels would require 100 square miles to minimize the possibility that the one submarine would fall upon another. About one-fourth of the 4000 tons of metal per submarine would be lost in land disposal through burial of the reactor compartment, whereas the whole amount would be lost in sea disposition.

For all three options there was no identifiable impact upon ecology, although in ocean disposal, the distribution of life might be altered by organisms seeking shelter near the hulls.

The individual exposure levels were all derived using very conservative assumptions. For the land disposal of 100 reactor compartments, 0.006 millirem constituted the individual exposure. For the sinking of 100 submarines at sea followed by considerable corrosion, 0.0002 millirem would be the individual exposure. Occupational exposures higher than those for the general public would be had by shipyard and naval personnel. A value of 18 man-rem per disposal is calculated. For protective storage, 3 man-rem might be received by an individual worker.

The estimated costs for the disposal options are provided below. The application of 20 years of protective custody would increase the cost of disposal through either option by three million dollars.

Estimated costs of disposing of one submarine in 1981 dollars:

Bury reactor compartment and salvage remainder of submarine:
  13.3 million

Bury reactor compartment and sink remainder of submarine at sea:
7.2 million
Sea disposal of entire submarine: 5.2 million

The Navy's Draft Environmental Impact Statement was circulated to over 1500 individuals, environmental organizations and public officials. Five hundred comments were received over a six-month period. Most of the letters were directed against the ocean disposal option, with arguments that there existed inadequate information to assess the proposed disposition. However, most of the written perceptions were not in accord with data in the impact statement and with existing engineering and scientific wisdom. Concerns were also expressed about the Navy's ability to monitor at sea, retrieval capabilities and about the possible entry of radioactivity into the human food chain.

The Navy responded to the political, economic and environmental information with acceptance of the land burial option. US Congress and the Environmental Protection Agency were unsympathetic toward ocean disposal. Thus, contrary to a strong economic bias and to sound environmental arguments for ocean disposal, there were social and political considerations that led to a decision for land disposal.

The British Ministry of Defence looks with favour upon the sea disposal of its eight to ten nuclear submarines whose useful life will end by the beginning of the twenty-first century (Mar. Poll., 1989b). The arguments in favour are primarily economic. Burial is proposed at water depths two miles below the surface. One decommissioned submarine remains in storage with its reactor core and fuel rods having been removed.

Overview

Marine scientists and engineers in advanced societies possess or can obtain appropriate information for the marine disposal of some societal wastes and in some areas. The current perceptions of governmental bodies, strongly influenced by environmental groups, view the use of the oceans as waste space as being heretical. National and international policies are foreclosing today upon the ocean disposal options.

Increasing populations, coupled with dwindling land disposal sites, will bring into play the economics of the problem. Furthermore, comparative risk assessments of disposal options by natural and social scientists and by engineers may lead nations back to the oceans.

References

Barkatt, S., Saad, E. E., Adiga, R., Sousanpour, W., Barkatt, A., Al., Adel-Hadadi, M. A., O'Keefe, J. A. and Alterescu, S. Leaching of natural and nuclear waste glasses in seawater. *Appl. Geochem.* 4, 593–603 (1989).

Black, D. Investigation of possible increased incidence of cancer in West Cumbria. Her Majesty's Stationery Office, London. 104 p. (1984).

Blus, L. J., Gish, C. D., Belise, A. A. and Pourty, R. M. Logarithmic relationship of DDE residues to eggshell thinning. *Nature* 235, 376–7 (1972).

Bruce, M. The London Dumping Convention, 1972: First Decade and Future. *In: Ocean Yearbook* 6, eds. E. M. Borgese and N. Ginsburg. University of Chicago Press, Chicago, pp. 298–318 (1986).

Capuzzo, J. M. and Lancaster, B. A. Zooplankton population response to individual wastes discharged at Deepwater Dumpsite 106. *In:* Wastes in the Ocean, Vol. 5. *Deep Sea Waste Disposal.* Eds. D. Kester *et al.* John Wiley and Sons, New York. pp. 209–26 (1985).

Carson, Rachel. *Silent Spring.* Houghton-Mifflin, Boston (1962).

Cons. Ex. How do U.S. multinationals handle hazardous wastes abroad? *Conservation Exchange,* 6, 3 (1988).

Cottam, C. and E. Higgins. DDT: Its effects on fish and wildlife. U.S. Dept. Int., Fish Wildl. Serv. Circ. II, 14 p. (1946).

Davies, Gareth. Deep-Sea Sludge Disposal. *Mar. Poll. Bull.* 20, 104 (1989).

EPA (1990). Characteristics of municipal solid wastes in the United States: 1990 update. U.S. EPA/530-SW-90-042. Washington D.C. 103 p. plus appendices.

Epstein, J. Rate of decomposition of GB in seawater. *Science* 170, 1396–8 (1970).

Farrington, J. W., Goldberg, E. D., Risebrough, R. W., Martin, J. H. and Bowen, V.T. U.S. 'Mussel Watch' 1976-1978. An overview of the trace metal, DDE, PCB, hydrocarbon and artificial radionuclide data. *Environ. Sci. Technol.* 17, 490–60 (1983).

Goldberg, E. D. The mussel watch – a first step in global marine monitoring. *Mar. Poll. Bull.* 6, III (1975).

Goldberg, E. D. *The Health of the Oceans.* Unesco Press. Paris. 172 p. (1976).

Goldberg, E. D. Marine metal pollutants: a small set. *Mar. Poll. Bull.* 25, 45 (1992).

Goldberg, E. D. (ed.). *Assimilative Capacity of U.S. Coastal Waters for Pollutants.* U.S. Department of Commerce. National Oceanic and Atmospheric Administration. Environmental Research Laboratories. Boulder, Colorado. 184 p. (1979).

Grassle, F. Sludge reaching bottom at the 106 site, not dispersing as plan predicted. *Oceanus* 33, 6, 6–2 (1990).

Hallegraeff, G. M. Toxic dinoflagellate blooms in Australian waters. *In:* IOC Workshop Report No. 47. Annex II, p. 12 (1987).

Hollister, C. D., Anderson, D. R. and Health, G. R. Subseabed disposal of nuclear wastes. *Science* 213, 1321–26 (1981).

Hunt, G. J. Radioactivity in Surface and Coastal Waters of the British Isles, 1987. Aquatic Environmental Monitoring Report Number 19. Lowestoft. 67 p. (1988).

IOC. IOC Workshop on International Cooperation in the Study of Red Tides and Ocean Blooms. Workshop Report No. 57 (1987).

Jackson, G. A. Sludge Disposal in Southern California Basins. *Environ. Sci. Techn.* 16, 746–57 (1982).

Jenkenson, I. R. Red tides and toxic phytoplankton on the North and West coasts of France. IOC Workshop Report No. 57. p. 19 (1987).

Kasoulides, G. C. Ban on marine incineration. *Mar. Poll. Bull.* 19, 648 (1988).

Linnenbom, V. J. Final Report on First Post-Dump Survey of the Chase X Disposal Site. U.S. Naval Research Laboratory Memorandum Report 2273, 11 p. (1971).

MAFF. Ministry of Agriculture, Fisheries and Food, Directorate of Fisheries Research. First Report of the Marine Monitoring Management Group's Coordinating Group on Monitoring of Sewage Sludge Disposal Sites. Lowestoft, United Kingdom. 64 p. (1989).

MAFF. Ministry of Agriculture, Fisheries and Food, Directorate of Fisheries Research. Radioactivity in Surface and Coastal waters of the British Isles, 1989. Aquatic Environment Monitoring Report 23, 66 p. (1990).

MAFF. Ministry of Agriculture, Fisheries and Food, Directorate of Fisheries Research. Second Report of the Marine Pollution Monitoring Management Group's Coordinating Group on Monitoring of Sewage Sludge Disposal Sites. Lowestoft, United Kingdom, 39 p. (1991*a*).

MAFF. Ministry of Agriculture, Fisheries and Food, Directorate of Fisheries Research. Third Report of the Marine Pollution Monitoring Management Group's Coordinating Group on Monitoring of Sewage Sludge Disposal Sites. Lowestoft, United Kingdom, 37 p. (1991*b*).

Mar. Poll. Convention on dumping at sea. *Mar. Poll. Bull.* 3, 177–8 (1972).

Mar. Poll. Radwaste at Sea. *Mar. Poll. Bull.* 16, 2 (1985).

Mar. Poll. Organosilicon compounds: dumping convention changes. *Mar. Poll. Bull.* 18, 99–101 (1986).

Mar. Poll. Oslo/Paris Commission. *Mar. Poll. Bull.* 14, 46–78 (1987).

Mar. Poll. Ocean Disposal of Radioactive wastes to be studied. *Mar. Poll. Bull.* 19, 198 (1988).

Mar. Poll. Sludge Dumping - Pressure on UK Mounts. *Mar. Poll. Bull.* 20, 363 (1989*a*).

Mar. Poll. Plans to dump nuclear subs at sea. *Mar. Poll. Bull.* 20, 251 (1989*b*).

Mar. Poll. North Sea becomes MARPOL Special Area. *Mar Poll. Bull.* 22, 218–19 (1991).

NAS. *Our Seabed Frontier.* National Academy Press. Washington D.C., xvii + 138 p. (1990).

NAS. *Disposal of Industrial and Domestic Wastes, Land and Sea Alternatives.* National Academy Press. Washington D.C. 210 p. (1984).

Navy. Final Environmental Impact Statement on the Disposal of Decommissioned, Defueled Naval Submarine Reactor Plants. 3 Vols. U.S. Department of the Navy. Washington D.C. (1984).

NOAA. Scientific Problems Relating to Ocean Pollution. Environmental Research Laboratories, U.S. National Oceanics and Atmospheric Administration, Boulder, Colorado, 225 p. (1979).

Norton, M. G. The Oslo and London Dumping Conventions. *Mar. Poll. Bull.* 12, 145–9 (1981).

NYT. *New York Times,* 18 July 1990.

Peet, G. London Dumping Convention: Obsolete or Effective. *Mar. Poll. Bull.* 22, 56–8 (1991).

Pomiankowski, A. Cancer incidence in Sellafield. *Nature* 311, 100 (1984).

Preston, A. The radiological consequences of releases from nuclear facilities to the aquatic environment. *In: Impacts of Nuclear Releases to the Aquatic Environment.* International Atomic Energy Agency, Vienna. pp. 3–23 (1975).

Redford, D., Jackson, M., Gentile, J., Oberacker, D., Boehm, P. and Werme, C. Assessing Potential Effects of Incinerating Organic Wastes at Sea. *Mar. Poll. Bull.* 19, 599–601 (1988).

Rosenberg, R. Negative oxygen trends in Swedish coastal bottom waters. *Mar. Poll. Bull.* 21, 335–9 (1990).

Side, J. The European Community and Dumping at Sea. *Mar. Poll. Bull.* 17, 290–4 (1986).

Smayda, T. J. Primary production and the global epidemic of phytoplankton blooms in the sea: A link? *In: Novel Phytoplankton Blooms,* ed. E. M. Cosper, V. M. Bicelj and E. J. Carpenter. Springer Verlag, New York, pp. 449–83 (1989).

Smayda, T. Novel and nuisance phytoplankton blooms in the sea: evidence for a global epidemic. *In: Toxic Marine Phytoplankton,* eds. E. Graneli *et al.,* Elsevier Science Publishing, pp. 29–40 (1990).

Vir, A. K. Toxic trade with Africa. *Environ. Sci. Technol.* 23, 23–5 (1989).

Wolfe, D. A. Persistent plastics and debris in the ocean: An international problem of ocean disposal. *Mar. Poll. Bull.* 18, 303–5 (1987).

Farming and ranching the sea

The cultivation of plants and animals of the sea is enjoying rapid and successful growth at the present time. As a result, the products compete in price with those from the wild. The contribution of farmed fish and shellfish to that of their wild counterparts will increase in the future as a result of economic forces and of genetic engineering. Yet, the activities can have negative impacts upon marine systems, including diminishing environmental quality and competition with natural populations for food. The problems at both national and international levels require the formulation of regulations where they do not exist, and continuing modification of those that are already enacted in the face of rapidly changing developments.

Introduction

The remarkable and economically successful growth of mariculture, ocean farming and ranching is placing increasing demands upon coastal space and resources. Aquaculture, which encompasses activities in both fresh and salt waters, accounts for about 10 per cent of the world harvest of fish and shellfish (Rhodes, 1989). It is dominated by freshwater finfish culture, but marine activities are clearly on the rise (Table 4.1 and Fig. 4.1). For example, the cultivation of crustaceans increased nearly ten-fold worldwide between 1975 and 1985.

Genetic engineering promises to increase the efficiency of fish farming and the amount of produce in the very near future (Fischetti, 1991). In the mid-

*Table 4.1. Aquaculture production by region
and country, 1988 (metric tons)*

Region	No. countries	Finfish	Crustacea	Mollusca	Seaweeds	Others
Africa, North & NE	4	57,733	2	530	0	0
Africa, S. of Sahara	34	11,328	75	232	0	50
North America	2	260,160	30,675	131,888	0	0
Central America	8	9,333	8,612	52,031	0	0
South America	12	22,326	87,928	316	23,109	0
Caribbean	12	17,053	1,343	1,541	4	30
Europe	29	472,008	3,042	621,432	0	2
USSR	1	359,549	0	234	5,000	0
Near East	11	33,455	13	0	0	0
Oceania	10	3,989	564	34,700	629	140
East Asia	10	4,863,142	337,271	2,114,958	3,526,077	33,781
West Asia	11	1,004,521	142,675	115,343	77,462	20
TOTAL		7,114,597	612,200	3,073,205	3,632,281	34,023
Percentage of world total		49.2	4.2	21.2	25.1	0.2

(Source: FAO, Aquaculture Minutes, No. 8, August 1990: taken from *Aq. Mag*
(1990).

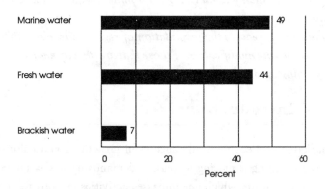

*Figure 4.1. International aquaculture production by
environment source: FAO Aquaculture Minutes No. 8.
Taken from* Aq. Mag. *(1990).*

1980s synthetic growth hormones were first fed to fish, inducing weight gains twice those of controls. But the economics were against this approach inasmuch as the synthetic hormones were expensive and the efficiency of uptake was low. Fish cloned genes that enhance the normal production of hormones were then used and the results of these researches are still under assessment. Consideration is also being given to incorporating into fish genes codes for anti-viral activity, for freezing avoidance, and for altering the male/female ratios of broods. Such work is in its infancy (Fischetti, 1991), yet does hold great promise.

In 1988, the global aquaculture product was $22.5 billion divided up as follows: China, $8 billion; Japan, $4.5 billion, and the United States $0.6 billion (Conrad, 1991a). The maricultured products from the basis of a strong export market in many countries. The nations that are major producers may not, however, be the major exporters (Table 4.2). The remarkable rise in the aquaculture industry in the western world can be seen in the Canadian example where large-scale activities began in the 1950s with trout and oyster cultivation (Patton, 1991). Expansion to grow salmon, mussels, Arctic char, scallops and certain marine plants continues to occur, and crop values grew from 7 million dollars annually in 1984 to 145 million in 1989. At the present time it is predicted that production could rise from 3 per cent of the landed value in 1990 to 25 per cent or more by the year 2000.

Table 4.2. Statistics on bivalve mariculture, 1987 (Mollusc Farming, 1990)

	Clams	Mussels	Oysters
Major producer	China	Spain	Rep. Korea
Amount in million tons	889,951	206,706	303,223
Major exporter	China	Netherlands	Rep. Korea
Amount in million tons	13,483	45,668	6,288
Major importer	Japan	France	United States
	Thailand		

Hybrid striped bass is one of several organisms being intensely studied as a new entry into mariculture. Other entries include sturgeon, soft-shelled crab, halibut, abalone, marron and additional species of algae (*Aq. Mag*, 1990).

There are two classes of mariculture: farming and ranching. In the former case, the organisms are maintained in enclosures of one type or another – pens, enclosed or semi-enclosed basins, etc. – with the farmer usually providing their food. In the latter, young fish are introduced into rivers or estuaries from which they enter the open ocean, naturally existing prey primarily offering sustenance to the fish.

Four types of mariculture exemplify and dominate the growing economic force of this activity: seaweed, shrimp, mussels and salmon (Table 4.3). Asia is the major culturing region for seaweed, with the principal use being for human consumption (Rhodes, 1989). Japan is the largest producer, followed by the Republic of Korea, the Philippines and China.

Shrimp have become one of the most valuable of the maricultured organisms. Twenty-six per cent of the world's supply comes from farming with a harvest of 565,000 tons in 1989, up from the 1988 value of 480,000 tons (Fig. 4.2; WSF, 1990*b*). The Asian region produces the largest quantity of marine shrimp, followed by Latin America. The People's Republic of China, Indonesia, Thailand and the Philippines are the major producers in Asia, and Ecuador in Latin America (Table 4.4). The producing countries used up about 15 per cent of the 1989 crop; the remainder went to the United States, Europe and Japan (WSF, 1990*b*). The sensitivity of the export trade to a single country can be seen in a recent episode. A price crash of frozen shrimp in 1988–89 has been attributed to a cutback in the consumption of festival luxury food in Japan during Emperor Hirohito's prolonged illness in 1988, a period in which celebrations were frowned upon.

The statistics of the People's Republic of China provide an illuminating example of shrimp mariculture in the developing world. Whilst aquaculture accounts for 42 per cent of the total fisheries industry, 11 to 12 per cent encompasses mariculture in ponds or cages. Of this, 4 per cent involves the production of shrimp, a practice which is expanding to meet the demands of the world market (Forbes, 1990). Marine culture of shrimp takes up between fifteen and twenty thousand hectares of space.

As a result of such activities on a global basis, the price of shrimp in the world marketplace has declined. The farmed shrimp now represent about 26 per cent of the world harvest compared with 2.1 per cent in 1981 (Fig. 4.2). There is a sense that with time farmed shrimp will totally displace wild shrimp as articles of commerce. The shrimp fishermen today constitute an endangered species.

The amount of shrimp produced per unit area depends upon the strategies followed (WSF, 1990*b*). For extensive shrimp farming as practised in the tropics, the farmer gathers his crop of young shrimp from adjacent waters and cultures them to maturity. To a large extent the shrimp feed on naturally occurring organisms; in some cases plant fertilizers are added. Harvest of 50 to 500 kg/hectare are usual.

In semi-intensive mariculture, the juveniles are raised under high density conditions in nursery ponds and transferred later to lower density grow-out ponds. Yields range from 500 to 5000 kg/hectare.

In intensive shrimp mariculture, high stocking densities, small enclosures,

Table 4.3. FAO Aquaculture species production, 1988*

Category	Metric tons
Carps, barbels and other cyprinids	4,589,078
Tilapias and other cichlids	264,535
Miscellaneous freshwater fishes	1,071,680
Sturgeons, paddlefishes	205
River eels	99,080
Salmons, trouts, smelts	459,233
Miscellaneous diadromous fishes	349,298
Flounders, halibuts, soles	3,280
Cods, hakes, haddocks	7
Redfishes, basses, congers	53,795
Jacks, mullets, sauries	187,120
Herrings, sardines, anchovies	3
Tunas, bonitos, billfishes	47
Miscellaneous marine fishes	34,236
Freshwater crustaceans	59,650
Sea-spiders, crabs	3,303
Lobsters, spiny-rock lobsters	90
Shrimps, prawns	511,454
Miscellaneous marine crustaceans	33,941
Freshwater molluscs	2,130
Abalones, winkles, conchs	1,598
Oysters	997,155
Mussels	1,029,354
Scallops, pectens	305,529
Clams, cockles, arkshells	456,592
Miscellaneous marine molluscs	284,609
Frogs and other amphibians	20
Turtles	845
Sea-squirts and other tunicates	32,519
Miscellaneous aquatic invertebrates	427
Pearls, mother-of-pearl, shells	212
Sponges	0
Brown seaweeds	2,366,994
Red seaweeds	850,020
Green seaweeds and other algae	8,670
Miscellaneous aquatic plants	406,597
TOTAL	14,466,306

*Includes catfish

FAO Fisheries Circular No. 815 Revision 2.

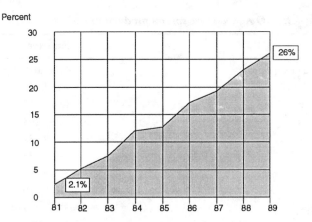

Percent

Figure 4.2. World production of farm-raised shrimp as percentage of world shrimp harvest (WSF, 1990b)

heavy feed, waste removal and aeration combine to yield 5000 to 10,000 kg/ hectare. More closely controlled farming, super-intensive and still experimental, may produce 10,000 to 100,000 kg/hectare. The high costs of such farming place it in a high-risk category. Much of the farming in the developing world is extensive, although China has a unique semi-intensive activity.

Western Europe is the major producer of farmed salmon. Norway accounts for nearly ninety per cent of the world's production, followed by the United Kingdom (Scotland and the Orkney and Shetland Islands) (Rhodes, 1989). In the latter development, future expansion will probably come about at existing sites, since desirable areas in coastal waters have been essentially exhausted. In the former case, the potential production is perhaps 700,000 tons per year (Conrad, 1991b). European farmed salmon production was predicted to increase from the annual 60,000 tons in 1986 to 140,000 to 260,000 tons in 1990 (Table 4.4).

In salmon farming the fry are hatched from eggs and grown in troughs, tanks or raceways. They are then transferred to cages in fresh waters and are grown until they are ready for entry to cages or tanks with saltwater. This takes about thirty months. At this time they are called smolts. In the saltwaters their growth rates are much higher and they reach marketable weights of 1.5– 2.0 kg (grilse). With a further year's growth they achieve weights of 2–3 kg for the males and 5 kg for the females.

In salmon ranching, the effectiveness depends upon the ability of the fish to return to the release site after spending time in the open ocean, sometimes at distances of thousands of kilometres. A 1 per cent return represents the break-even point; in practice 1 to 2 per cent or more has been observed (Lowe, 1988).

Yet the economic attractiveness of mariculture has its detractions.

Table 4.4. European farmed salmon production (in tons) (NCC, 1989)

	1986	1990
Scotland	10,400	25,000–32,000
Norway	45,500	100,000–200,000
Iceland + Faroes	2,000	4,000–10,000
Ireland	1,500	10,000–15,000
France	500	1,000–2,000
	60,000	140,000–259,000

Overproduction has threatened expansion in some areas (Fin. Times, 1989). For example, the surge in the output of Norwegian salmon reduced the minimum price, regulated by the Norwegian Fish Farmers Sales Organization, by 16 per cent in 1989. Competition is so great that fish are often sold below the cost of production. In Japan farmed salmon claimed a larger share of the market than those captured in the wild (Fig. 4.3). As a consequence the salmon fishermen suffered employment losses.

Aquaculture is an important supplier of fish and shellfish in the United States (Table 4.6). Although over half of the value of the products are freshwater catfish with a value of $380 million in 1988, mariculture provides a substantial contribution in the remainder. Overall aquaculture accounts for 6.5 per cent of the US edible fish and is growing at an average rate of 12.5 per cent annually.

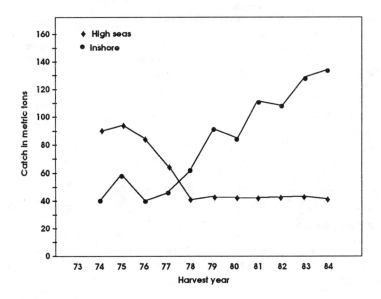

Figure 4.3. The comparison between the production of salmon by farming (inshore) and the wild catch (high seas) in Japan. From Isaksson, 1988.

Table 4.5. World aquaculture of shrimp in 1989 (SSF, 1990)

Country by rank	% of world production	Hands-on production	Hectares in production	Kilograms per hectare
China	29	165,000	145,000	1,138
Indonesia	16	90,000	250,000	360
Thailand	16	90,000	80,000	1,125
Philippines	9	50,000	200,000	250
Ecuador	8	45,000	70,000	643
Vietnam	5	30,000	160,000	187
India	4	25,000	60,000	416
Taiwan	4	20,000	4,000	5,000
Central America and Caribbean	2	12,000	12,000	1,000
South America (excluding Ecuador)	1	7,000	8,000	875
Other	5	30,800	103,300	298
TOTALS	–	564,800	1,092,300	517
Eastern Hemisphere	89	500,100	1,002,300	499
Western Hemisphere	11	64,700	90,200	717

Table 4.6. Edible fishery products in the United States ($ billion) (Aq. Mag., 1989)

US Supply	1988	Estimate 1989	Estimate 1995	Average annual growth rate 1988-1995
Imports	5.46	5.28	5.72	0.7
US commercial landings	3.36	3.46	5.84	8.2
US aquaculture	0.58	0.59	0.90	6.5
US processed fishery product	5.04	5.14	7.04	4.9
The market for fish and seafood				
Export	2.16	2.76	3.90	8.8
Retail, food service and food stores	12.97	13.46	20.30	6.6
TOTAL	15.13	16.22	24.20	6.9

Problems with mariculture

Both ranching and farming of marine organisms, like their equivalents on land, have self-generated and imposed impediments to success.

First of all, the activities can compete for coastal ocean space with transportation, recreation and waste disposal sites. Secondly, continued expansion and existing practices can jeopardize the quality of the environment and result in the loss of resources (NCC, 1989).

In the case of ranching a primary concern involves the deliberate or accidental interception of cultured fish. In both the Atlantic and Pacific there are charges of the poaching of ranched salmon. Usually the interceptors are from countries other than that of the maricultural activity.

Perhaps more distressing is the loss of ranched fish through illegal drift netting on the open seas, using 3-inch mesh nylon nets that may be up to 40 miles long and 40 feet in depth (Lenssen, 1990), which can remove tremendous numbers of fish from the areas they sweep. The salmon run failures in 1987 and 1988 have been attributed to this activity and 100 million salmon, worth about one billion dollars were lost by the US enterprise alone.

Finally, there is the unintentional capture of the ranched fish during the recovery of other organisms. A recent case involved the gill-netting of squid and the simultaneous entanglement of ranched salmon. The catches are made primarily by fishermen from Japan, the Republic of Korea and Taiwan (Time, 1989). In addition these nets are often lost at sea where they can entangle organisms that cross their paths, the so-called ghost fishing. Consequently fewer salmon return to the US coastal areas for spawning. Bilateral agreements between the United States and Japan have been negotiated in which US observers are placed upon about 10 per cent of Japan's 3350 squid-catching vessels to determine the number of fish taken in the nets. No agreements have as yet been made with the Republic of Korea and Taiwan.

Maricultural activities may have both positive and negative effects upon natural populations that come into contact with the farms (NCC, 1989). First of all, the area of the enclosures offers to wild fish a novel environment in which there is food (the uneaten materials from the caged fish and the encrusting plant and animal growths on the structures) and protection.

The fishmeal requirements in the diet of the farmed products are high. For example, one ton of dry fish meal is required to produce one ton of salmon. Salmon mariculture uses up five per cent of the United Kingdom fish meal production. Although at the present time there appears to be no impact on the fish involved in fish meal production, some have been involved in problems of overfishing. Expansion of salmon mariculture could in principle put pressure on endangered stocks (NCC, 1989).

Environmental quality

There are a number of general problems generated by the mariculture itself.

Competition with natural populations

In the case of ranching there is the haunting problem of the competition for food between herded organisms and wild species. Fish ranchers clearly wish to utilize the carrying capacity of the oceans (i.e. the abundance of prey) for their organisms. How to ascertain whether or not it has been exceeded is a most difficult task. Increasing salmon releases to the Columbia River are associated with declining adult returns (Isaksson, 1988). Also the Atlantic may be supporting a smaller salmon population today than it did in the 1700s. Whether these phenomena reflect overwhelmingly the carrying capacity of the oceans or other factors is not as yet established.

Genetic contamination

Rivers indoctrinate their salmon with some chemical characteristics that are transferred from one generation to the next. The inherited factors provide a means for the salmon to return to a specific river after spending time in the open ocean. Pen bred stock through selective breeding may not maintain this identifying ability in their genetic makeup. In a report to the Nature Conservancy Council by P. S. Maitland, the suggestion is made that 'Hatchery fish can depress the number and performance of wild fish when the former are released to the wild in large numbers'. Inadvertent or deliberate release of farmed salmon is alleged to take place and to create the potential problem.

Loss of natural habitats

Another impact of farming upon the coastal ocean is the loss of natural habitats. For example, the depletion of mangrove forests, a valuable but declining ecosystem, is associated with shrimp farming in the Southeast Pacific (Aqua, 1989). In Panama an areal loss of one per cent per year is the reported rate. In Ecuador, 60,000 of the 177,000 hectares of mangroves have already been turned over to salt water shrimp farming. However, in south-east Asia there is a mitigating factor. The acid-sulphate soils which are associated with mangroves, are detrimental to shrimp mariculture and thus many of the activities have moved inland.

Impacts with waste disposal

The entry of domestic and industrial wastes can seriously affect maricultured organisms living near the receiving waters. High levels of plant nutrients, such as nitrate and phosphate, and organic materials associated with the wastes, can lead to eutrophication and the population bursts of toxic organisms, the so-called red tides.

A dramatic example involves the largest bay in Korea, Jinhae Bay, which is the home of an extensive mariculture activity involving oysters and brown and red algae (Cho, 1991). The waters receive large amounts of phosphates from a fertilizer plant as well as from municipal discharges. Seventy per cent of the maricultured products come from Jinhae Bay; the products have increased eight fold in the decades between 1968 and 1988 and represent increases of 11.6 to 27.6 of the total fisheries production. The combination of wastes from mariculture and sewerage have combined to produce red tides of flagellates which devastated the oyster crops in 1978 and 1981, valued at 4.5 and 2.25 US million dollars respectively. The frequency of the tidal events is continuously increasing.

Mass mortalities of aquacultured Chinese prawns (*Penaeus orientalis*) and bay scallops (*Argopecten irradians*) were experienced in farms on the northern coast of China in the summer of 1990 (Wu, 1991), the problem being attributed to the discharge of industrial wastes from paper mills, pesticide plants and plastic manufacturers.

A recent case of pollution in Taiwan emphasizes the use of maricultural activities as pollution sentinels, similar to the story of tributyl tin. The episode occurred in the maricultural area of Taiwan (Han and Hung, 1990). In 1986 a green coloration of oysters, both maricultured and wild, was observed off the west coast of the island, with mortalities noted about three months later. Copper was the alleged culprit. The source of the copper involved a local recycling operation, the conduit to the estuarine area where the important oyster farming takes place being the Erhjin Chi River.

It should be pointed out that although lead and cadmium were not enriched in the organisms, zinc displayed a similar behaviour to copper. The correlation coefficient between these two metals in the organisms was 0.89 (Hung and Tsai, 1991). Whether we are concerned with copper pollution or zinc pollution or some combination of the two is not as yet clear.

The present feeling among marine chemists is that copper in seawater is nearly completely associated with organic ligands, as yet unidentified (Moffett *et al.*, 1990). Like tin and mercury, the entry of copper to the biosphere is enhanced by an association with organic groups.

Therapeutants and non-target organisms

Marine mariculture is a form of monoculture and as such is subject to crop failures due to the invasion of predators, especially microorganisms. For example, the 1988 black tiger shrimp devastation in Taiwan may have been a consequence of such a phenomenon.

The inhibition of such disasters is sought with therapeutants such as the powerful antibiotics tetracycline and streptomycin. These pharmaceuticals are introduced with the feed or directly to the waters of the cage. In the latter case cages are raised from the bottom to give an effective depth of several metres and water movement is restricted by tarpaulins about the enclosure. For example, an anti-chlorinesterase agent, Duvan, is used in the control of sea lice on penned salmon (Ross, 1989). Its concentration in the waters is brought to about 1 ppm and the fish are exposed for about an hour. Canadian studies indicate that at this concentration it is not toxic to mussels or periwinkles after one hour exposure, but is toxic to larval lobsters, adult lobsters, zooplankton and phytoplankton (Cusack and Johnson, 1990). In spite of heavy use in the United Kingdom salmon from 43 retail outlets in the southeastern areas showed no contamination by this compound in 1990 (*Mar. Poll. Bull.*, 1991). On the other hand, the potential impact on non-target organisms near treatment sites has resulted in a prohibition of its use in Canada (Cusack and Johnson, 1990). The continued development of fish farming clearly should be matched with field and laboratory studies of therapeutant impacts upon non-target organisms in the farming area.

Anti-foulants have been applied to pens, both the structures and the nets, in order to minimize the build-up of organisms. Copper-containing compounds and tributyl tins have been used. The extreme toxicity of the latter, coupled with its discovery in the flesh of salmon grown in Scotland caused the government to ban its use. The concern related to public health although there is no evidence that the ppm levels of the anti-foulant in the edible parts of the fish jeopardized the health of humans.

Alterations of the quality of the water column

Marine farming can alter water quality by the introduction of nutrients from waste products and through the decomposition of food with the consequential growth of algae. Yet there is little definitive evidence for the increase of primary productivity near fish cages (NCC, 1989). There are scattered reports in the literature of plankton blooms associated with fish farms. These problems are in need of continuous monitoring and research.

The creation of anoxic environments

Fish farming in cages or with rafts produces organic residues from uneaten food and from the metabolic wastes. These materials sink to the bottom and through microbial decomposition release the dissolved biostimulants, such as phosphate, nitrate, silicate and ammonia, to the waters. Enhanced plant growth in the water column can come about and serious pollution problems can develop. For example, Hong Kong Island has degraded environments under rafts which occupy waters in what were once some of the cleanest and most beautiful areas (Morton, 1989). This situation has disturbed the Hong Kong Yachting Association, which represents user communities who desire the space for canoeing, windsurfing, motorboating, swimming, sailing, snorkeling and scuba diving. Mariculture accounts for 50 per cent of the total live fish consumption in Hong Kong and has an annual value of $25 million.

Benthic communities are especially sensitive to changes as a consequence of the accumulation of uneaten food and metabolic wastes under fish farm pens. As the trend toward anoxia takes place, there are alterations in community structure such that organisms with shells are replaced by organisms without shells, polychaetes for example (Tsutsumi *et al.*, 1991). The Japanese workers have charted population changes below a red sea-bream farm in Tomioka Bay as the chemical make-up of the benthos tended toward anoxia since 1966 to the present.

Oxygen depletion in the bottom waters were observed each summer since 1978 with a consequential but temporary disappearance of benthic animals at this time. High levels of sulphides appeared in the sediments. In 1966 molluscs accounted for 70 to 98 per cent of the animal population. By 1989, there was a numerical dominance of polychaetes which ranged between 50 and 90 per cent within the Bay.

On the other hand, the intense raft culture of mussels in northwest Spain (about 0.1 million tons per year) has an overall positive effect on the associated food chains (Tenore *et al.*, 1985). The faecal wastes of the mussels provide sustenance to demersal fish and crabs, although there has been a decrease in the diversity of benthic organisms in the area of the rafts. Scallop recruitment may be negatively affected.

To alleviate the problems of mariculture wastes upon natural populations the siting of cages for marine organisms in areas of strong tidal flow has been suggested (Frid and Mercer, 1989), whereas sea cages have generally been placed in sheltered zones with low tidal forces. Frid and Mercer studied the abundances of benthic organisms downstream of a salmon farm at Milford Haven, United Kingdom. Five species showed no significant changes in abundance going 45 m downstream from the farm. However, there does remain the concern that the long residence times of wastes in the waters can lead eventually to the stimulation of plankton blooms and eutrophication.

Introduction of alien species

Alien species may be introduced along with imported organisms for mariculture. For example, the continued spread in European waters of the brown seaweed *Sargassum muticum* came about through the importation to France of the Japanese oyster *Crassostrea gigas* (Rueness, 1989). The ecological impacts of such transplantations are difficult to predict. Some alien species have no impact upon the indigenous organisms, whereas others can displace natives, with potential impacts upon higher levels of the food web.

Then there is the perception that diseases in imported organisms are transported to their wild counterparts. Such is the case in South Carolina, USA where non-native imported shrimp were found in the wild (WSF, 1990a), some carrying the dreaded virus IHHNV. Whilst in experiments extending over six months the alien creatures were not found to transmit the microorganisms to the native species, the suspicion still persists.

Impacts on birds and mammals

Contained fish and shellfish provide an attractive food source for birds and for marine mammals. Farmers thus take countermeasures through anti-predator devices (traps and nets) and through shooting. In this war, there are financial losses to the farmer and ecological losses to the environmentalists. However, as yet these problems have not caused great concern (NCC, 1989).

There are a number of accusations against birds (NCC, 1989): they eat the products such as finfish and mussels; they damage fish making them less marketable and susceptible to disease; they dislodge mussels from their attachments; they spread disease; they introduce parasites; and their presence stresses fish, increasing susceptibility to disease and reducing their growth rates. Mammals such as seals, otters, minks and walruses, are also accused. The quantitative aspects of this problem have not as yet been addressed.

Management

The zooming expansion of maricultural practices at both national and international levels interferes with and can endanger competing coastal zone activities which themselves can impinge upon farming and ranching of the sea. The developments are so rapid that any policies should be framed with a high degree of flexibility. Possible lines of approach will be considered in Chapter 7.

The products of mariculture are coming under closer scrutiny, perhaps as a consequence of their profitable nature. For example, restrictions upon the sales of seaweeds based upon their toxicities are attributed to worldwide competition (IHT, 1990). Carrageenan, an extract of red seaweed, is used as a gelling, suspending and thickening agent in foods. Both the US Food and Drug Administration and the FAO have sought restrictions upon carrageenan containing more than 2 per cent acid insoluble matter or fibre content. Philippine producers were hit by this protocol, which they argued was inspired by US competitors.

An overriding fear of any monocultural activity, such as many maricultural pursuits, is the infestation by a microbe of one type or another. Some sense of the seriousness of a predator attack can be seen in the infection of oysters in the Gulf of Mexico by the protozoan *Perkinsus marinus* (Craig *et al.*, 1989). This parasite is estimated to be responsible for the 50 per cent mortality of the oyster population. The factors that influence infestation are dominated by salinity and include agricultural and industrial activity and the average annual temperature regime. At 49 sites, only one had had less than 50 per cent of its oysters infected.

The management strategies (Andrews and Ray, 1988) against this widespread disease occurring in the oyster reef animals can provide guidance to other mariculturists. For example, the protozoans flourish in high as opposed to low salinity regimes. Thus, the diversion of fresh waters into high-salinity bay systems can enhance oyster production there such that the average salinity is maintained above 15 per cent. Also, younger oysters appear more resistant to infection than older ones. Fall planted oysters can be harvested in the spring, if the legal minimum size limits are reduced. Siting of fish and shellfish farms can be effective where the ecologies of disease are known and can be utilized by the farmer.

The uneasiness of some facets of our society with mariculture recently surfaced in the Puget Sound area (Barinaga, 1990) with respect to salmon farming. Its critics were composed of fishermen, owners of waterfront property and the environmentalists. On the other side are the State of Washington officials who support this budding industry which can enhance the economy of the entire state. Where the Governor's office argue that farming of salmon is a clean activity, its opponents entertain a different view. They cite the arguments that the wastes of a 50,000 to 100,000-salmon pen in a two-acre area amount to 0.1 tons of uneaten food and faeces per year. This waste depletes oxygen in the water and sediments and kills bottom-living organisms of commercial value.

Similarly algal blooms, it is argued, poison marine life. Although direct relation-ships of farms to blooms have not been established, salmon deaths due to algae have forced many farms into bankruptcy (Barinaga, 1990). Diseases are associated with stock and eggs; a new disease for North America, viral haemorrhagic septicaemia, provides an argument for anti-farmers. Yet the relationship between disease and importation of viruses is yet to be established. Then there is the concern about therapeutants and the growth of antibiotic resistant bacteria. Most of the concerns are conceptual not substantative.

Although these arguments have been answered by the State with scientific data, the environmental activists continue to press their case. The scientists argue that careful management of the farms can avert any environmental damage; the environmental activists maintain the farms are a source of pollution. The stand-off continues.

The growth in the sales of maricultured fish, which exceeds the rate of population increase, supports the acceptance of the products by the general public. But are pen-grown salmon or mangrove-grown shrimp the equivalent of their wild counterparts? A discussion with noted chefs revealed differences (Time, 1990):

Chef Eberhard Mueller of Le Benardin, one of the best fish restaurants in New York, states wild salmon is much better for a marinade ... it stays firmer and has great intensity of flavour. Yet he concedes that farm-raised salmon is a very good product and it is easy to work with.

David Bouley, owner of a four-star restaurant that bears his name wouldn't even make stock from the carcasses, because the bones have an oily taste.

But the chefs do use some maricultured products such as scallops and oysters. Maricultured products can be moved from the enclosures to the restaurants rapidly. Sometimes the wild product can be treated in unsympathetic ways for the production of delectable fare, such as long periods of sitting at the dock. The verdict from Time (1990) is that farmed sea products are quite edible.

References

Andrews, J. D. and Ray, S. M. Management strategies to control the disease caused by *Perkinsus marinus*. *Amer. Fish. Soc. Spec. Publ.* 18, 257–64 (1988).

Aq. Mag. U.S. Fishery Industry Becoming Stronger. Aquaculture Mag. Nov./Dec., pp. 24–289 (1989).

Aq. Mag. Status of World Aquaculture 1990. *Aquaculture Mag. Buyers Guide,* pp. 6–14 (1990).

Aqua. Shrimp Farming in Southeast Asia. *Aquaculture Digest* 14, 5 (1989).

Barinaga, M. Fish, money and science in Puget Sound. *Science* 247, 631 (1990).

Cho, Chang-Hwan. Mariculture and eutrophication in Jinhae Bay, *Korea. Mar. Poll. Bull.* 23, 275–9 (1991).

Conrad, J. FAO's birds-eye view of aquaculture. *Aquaculture Mag.* March-April, pp. 32–8 (1991*a*).

Conrad, J. How's the Norwegian salmon industry doing? *Aquaculture Mag.* May-June pp. 32–5 (1991*b*).

Craig, A., Powell, E. N., Fay, R. R. and Brooks, J. Distribution of *Perkinsus marinus* in Gulf Coast oyster populations. *Estuaries* 12, 82–91 (1989).

Cusack, R. and Johnson, G. A study of *dichlorvos* (Uvan 2, 2 *dichloroethenyl dimethyl* phosphate), a therapeutic agent for the treatment of salmonids infected with sea lice (*Lepeophtheirus salmonis*). *Aquaculture* 90, 101–2 (1990).

Fin. Times. *Financial Times,* London. 25 August (1989).

Fischetti, M. A feast of gene-splicing down on the fish farm. *Science* 253, 512–13 (1991).

Forbes, A. The shrimp industry in the People's Republic of China. *Aquaculture Mag.* Jan./Feb., pp. 44–8 (1990).

Frid, C. L. J. and Mercer, T. S. Environmental monitoring of caged fish farming in macrotidal environments. *Mar. Poll. Bull.* 20, 379–83 (1989).

Han, B. and Hung, T. Green oysters caused by pollution on the Taiwan coast. *Environ. Poll.* 65, 347–62 (1990).

Hodgkins, J. and Ho, K. C. Hong-Kong: Toxic red tides again. *Mar. Poll. Bull.* 22, 4 (1990).

Hung, T. and Tsai, C. Study of heavy metals on the western coast of Taiwan. Paper presented for Seminar on Physical and Chemical Oceanography. Hangzhou, China, 25–9 June (1991).

IHT (1990) *International Herald Tribune,* 3 July (1990).

Isaksson, A. Salmon ranching: A world review. *Aquaculture* 75, 1–33 (1988).

Lenssen, N. Casting off drift nets. *World Watch* 3, 6–7 (1990).

Lowe, M. D. Salmon ranching and farming net growing harvest. *World Watch* 2, 28–32 (1988).

Mar. Poll. Bull. Dichlorvos. *Mar. Poll. Bull.* 22, 55 (1990).

Moffett, J. W., Zika, R. G. and Brand, L. E. Distribution and potential sources and sinks of copper chelators in the Sargasso Sea. *Deep-Sea Research* 37, 27–36 (1990).

Mollusc Farming. International Trade in Mussels and Oysters. pp. 17–18 (1990).

Morton, B. Hong Kong's Pigs in the Sea. *Mar. Poll. Bull.* 20, 199–200 (1989).

NCC. Fish Farming and the Safeguard of the Natural Marine Environment of Scotland. Nature Conservancy Council. 236 p. (1989).

Patton, D. J. Canadian policies and program for coastal ocean space utilization. The Second International Symposium on Coastal Space Utilization. 2–4 April 1991. Long Beach, California USA (1991).

Rhodes, R. J. Status of World Aquaculture, 1988. *Aquaculture Magazine Buyers Guide.* pp. 6–20 (1989).

Ross, A. Nuvan use in salmon farming. *Mar. Poll. Bull.* 20, 373–4 (1989).

Rueness, J. *Sargassum muticum* and other introduced Japanese macroalgae: biological pollution of European coasts. *Mar. Poll. Bull.* 20, 173–6 (1989).

Tenore, K. R., Corral, J., Gonzalez, N. and Lopez-Jamar, E. Effect of intense mussel culture on food chain patterns and production in coastal Galacia, NW Spain. Proceedings of the International Symposium on the Utilization of Coastal Ecosystems: Planning, Pollution and Productivity, eds. Nig Labbish Chao and W. Kirby Smith. Rio Grande, Brazil (1985).

Time. Fish mining. *Time* (European Edition) 46, 29 May (1989).

Time. The fish tank on the farm. *Time* (US Edition) 46, 3 December (1990).

Tsai, C. C. H., Wu, S., Han, B. and Hung, T. Ecological and environmental studies along the copper recycling operation area: pollutant influence on biomass and primary productivity. *Acta. Ocean. Taiwanica* 21, 18–33 (1988).

Tsutsumi, H., Kikuchi, T., Tanaka, M., Higashi, T., Imasaka, K. and Miyazaki, M. Benthic faunal succession in a cove organically polluted by fish farming. *Mar. Poll. Bull.* 23, 233–8 (1991).

WSF. Shrimp Fishermen in South Carolina, U.S.A., Worry about Viruses from Farm Raised Shrimp. *World Shrimp Farming* 15, No. 9, 8 (1990a).

WSF. Chinese Shrimp Farming and its Problems. *World Shrimp Farming* 15, No. 7, 1–2 (1990b).

Wu, Bao Ling. Pollution has damaged coastal Aquaculture. *Mar. Poll. Bull.* 22, 371–2 (1991).

5. Transportation

Competition for space in coastal areas can be considered vertically as well as horizontally. If deep-port facilities are developed throughout the world to accommodate superfreighters, harbours will be deepened and subject to extensive and continuous dredging. Alterations to life processes in and surrounding the port area can be expected – fishing and nursery grounds of fish can be changed or eliminated. The dredging itself can interfere with sediment transport processes. Finally, increased ship loading and unloading can place additional stresses upon space in the port vicinity through the entry of alien materials and of non-indigenous organisms to the waters.

The use of undersea space for tunnels is now a reality. The longest ones include a 54 km tunnel, built between Honshu and Hokkaido in Japan and the 'Chunnel' beneath the English Channel connecting the United Kingdom with the European continent is nearing completion.

Introduction

The varying abilities of countries to produce articles of commerce, be they agricultural, industrial, medical or social, underlie the need for ready transport. The rising world population is demanding more materials and energy to achieve higher standards of living than those now experienced. For those countries producing or requiring the importation of high-volume, low-cost commodities such as coal, oil, timber and wheat, large-bulk ocean-traversing carriers (150,000 dwt or more) appear to be essential (NAS, 1985a). At the present time such vessels are primarily involved with the transport of petroleum and petroleum products.

Port facilities

The United States and the Mediterranean provide examples of the possible changes in harbour facilities that can come about as a result of changing economic conditions. In the former, the exportation of agricultural products and perhaps coal may provide an impetus for the construction of deep-water ports. Shifting industrialization in the Mediterranean from the northern to the southern and eastern countries will emphasize the need for improved harbour facilities (Grenon and Batisse, 1989), and ship movements will undoubtedly increase in the future.

In 1981 the United States had only three deep water ports, all located in California (Los Angeles, Long Beach and Richmond), capable of receiving large bulk carriers. Authorized depths of 47 feet or more are required to handle such large vessels. There are no active comparable ports on the East or Gulf Coasts, although a deep-water facility exists in Louisiana (Loop, Louisiana Offshore Port). On a world basis nearly all such ports are involved in the petroleum trade (Table 5.1; NAS, 1985b). The only Asian ports are Japanese and there are none in the developing nations of Africa. Yet it is these deep-water port deficient countries that may be in need of large quantities of low-bulk export in the future.

Cost-benefit analyses will determine whether or not the United States and other countries build deep-water ports. The costs of construction and maintenance are high. What will be the mix of materials than any given country will import and export, and how will such actions relate to the future world economy? Since any response involves predicting future economic trends, policy recommendations will be fraught with a high degree of uncertainty.

The present day ports in the United States reflect developments in the 1930s and 1940s (NAS, 1985a). They accommodate small vessels, the size of the Liberty and Victory ships constructed during World War II. Although containerized cargoes have altered the nature of port facilities, the volatility of the oil trade has not led to effective demands for more ports to handle supertankers.

The expense in constructing megaports will limit them to very small numbers. The criteria for upgrading existing ports will depend upon a number of factors. First of all, the facilities must interface with the land transportation system into which cargoes are fed. Are there adequate rail facilities? Can the associated highways accommodate the increased truck traffic and will the local citizens accept the accompanying noise? Are there appropriate terminal areas with associated storage facilities?

Table 5.1. World ports capable of handling vessels of 150,000 tons dwt or greater (NAS, 1985a)

Region/Country	Port
NORTH PACIFIC	
Japan:	Niigata, Mizushima, Kure, Kashima, Kimitsu, Chiba, Oita, Kitre, Tsurusaki, Okinawa, Tokyo Bay, Kawasaki, Yokkaichi
SOUTH PACIFIC	
Australia:	Port Hedlund, Dampier, Hay Point, Sydney Caves Beach, Clutha, Kembla, Bonython
NORTH AMERICA (excluding USA)	
Canada:	Seven Island, Come-by-Chance, St. John, Point Tupper, Roberts Bank
SOUTH AMERICA	
Venzuela:	Puerto La Cruz
Brazil:	Sepetiba, Tubarao
Chile:	Huasco
Peru:	San Nicolas
Argentina:	Bolivar
NORTH ATLANTIC	
Norway:	Narvik
Federal Republic of Germany:	Heligoland, Hamburg
United Kingdom:	Clyde Port, Glasgow, Tees-Port, Liverpool, Milford Haven, Port Talbot, Foulness
Ireland:	Bantry Bay
Spain:	Bilbao, Gijon, Algeciras
Sweden:	Gothenburg
France:	Dunkirk, Le Havre
Netherlands:	Rotterdam/Europoort
Belgium:	Zeebrugge, Antwerp
MEDITERRANEAN	
France:	Marseilles
Italy:	Trieste, Genoa, Taranto
Libyan Arab Jamahiriya:	Marsa el Brega
Egypt:	Port Said
PERSIAN GULF	
Islamic Rep. of Iran:	Kharp Island
Saudi Arabia:	Ras-al-Khafji, Ras Tanura
United Arab Emirates:	Das Island
Kuwait:	Mina-al-Ahmadi
AFRICA	
South Africa:	Richards Bay, Port Elizabeth, Algoa Bay, Saldanha Bay

Table 5.2. US import/export balance: exports minus imports
in millions of dollars (W. H. Branson, cited in NAS, 1985a)

Year	Agricultural goods	Fuels and lubricants	Chemicals	Capital goods	Consumer goods	Automotive products	Military goods	Other	Total
1930	−459	433	3	518	−92	282	7	−271	782
1937	−459	395	22	486	−38	353	22	−184	265
1947	1604	1013	553	3144	958	1147	174	890	9530
1960	857	−739	1128	4949	−505	633	804	−1226	5528
1970	558	−1384	2216	10557	−4834	−2242	1230	−3163	3303
1973	8023	−6359	3137	13928	−8481	−4543	1385	−5854	1863
1981	24308	−71333	11995	45680	−22864	−11750	3608	−11325	−27566

Changes in the US trade situation over the past half century can be seen in the dollar differences between exports and imports (Table 5.2). High technology products (chemicals and capital goods), coal, grains and timber presently constitute most of the exports. Forecasting the amounts of future exports is filled with uncertainty. Still, the NAS Report (1985a) concludes the United States should act expeditiously to increase its deep-water port facilities.

Present assessments suggest that North America (Canada and the United States) will be the major exporter of grains in the near future, primarily to Asia (Brown and Young, 1988). Asia has become a major importing region as a consequence of small and shrinking crop-land area per person (Table 5.3), whereas agricultural technologies promise to maintain the North American countries as producers. Such statistics provide compelling economic arguments for deep-water ports. However, the costs of increasing the physical capabilities of ports must be balanced against the gains from more competitive exports and the lesser costs for landing imports. Uncertainties in market changes, which take place over shorter times than those needed for deep-port construction, emphasize the risk factor in any assessment of deep-port needs.

Marine transportation in the Mediterranean reflects changing economic conditions in its industrialized and industrializing countries (Grenon and Batisse, 1989). Two aspects are of concern: hydrocarbon and bulk cargo transport. Whereas on a global basis, 36 per cent of the maritime transport encompasses petroleum and its derived products and liquefied natural gas, the comparable Mediterranean value is 50 per cent. The oil pollution problems there will be relatively high compared with most other marine waters.

About 20 per cent of the world's oil and oil products cargo passes through the Mediterranean. The amount of oil transported has been quite variable year by year, whereas there now appears to be a rather uniform rate of oil products transport.

Table 5.3. *World grain trade by region, 1950–88*[1]
(Brown and Young, 1988)

	1950	1960	1970	1980	1988[2]
N. America	23	39	56	131	119
L. America	1	0	4	−10	−11
W. Europe	−22	−25	−30	−16	22
E. Eur/USSR	0	0	0	−46	−27
Africa	0	−2	−5	−15	−28
Asia	−6	−17	−37	−63	−89
Aust/NZ	3	6	12	19	14

1. No sign indicates net exports, minus sign net imports.
2. Estimates.

The bulk goods transported include iron ore, coal and grain, less in value and in volume than oil and oil products (Grenon and Batisse, 1989). Steel production in northern European countries will probably decrease in the near future as a consequence of competition from the outside. Countries in the south and east Mediterranean, as part of their industrialization, will develop their activities with the importation of iron ore and coal. Large vessels will probably be employed and will enter ports that have appropriate draughts for the ships and suitable cargo handling facilities.

There can be unacceptable environmental impacts through the expansion of port facilities as a consequence of dredging operations, through the disposal of the dredge spoils and through the leakage to the waters from petroleum and petroleum products transport. The changes in the geometry of the harbour can affect its hydraulic regime. Circulation patterns can be altered with disturbances to the prevailing composition of the seawaters. The biological productivity of the harbour can be significantly affected. Deepening of the approach channels to Barrow-in-Furness in the United Kingdom produced 8 million tons of dredged materials in 1991, most of which were deposited at a single site off the southern tip of Walney Island (Aquat. Rep., 1993). An east-west transit of the area indicated that in the vicinity of the disposal site there were measurable contributions of the discharged materials and a reduced population or absence of large benthic species. The area will be continually monitored to ascertain whether or not there are persisting impacts.

The disposal of the dredged materials can pose substantial economic and social problems. Further, if they contain toxic materials there is the potential for adverse effects.

There are few examples in the literature treating the seriousness of toxic

Table 5.4. The invasion of marine organisms from one zone to another (Carlton and Geller, 1993)

Higher taxon	Taxon	Species	Native distribution	Intro-duced to	Year introduction first recognized (reference)
Dinoflagellata		*Alexandrium catenella*	Japan	Australia	1986
		Alexandrium minutum	Europe?	Australia	1986
		Gymnodinium catenatum	Japan	Australia	1986
Cnidaria	Scyphozoa	*Phyllorhiza punctata* (*, †)	Indo-Pacific	California	1981
	Hydrozoa	*Cladonema uchidai* (†)	Japan, China	California	1979
Ctenophora		*Mnemiopsis leidyi*	Western Atlantic	Black Sea	1987
Annelida	Oligochaeta	*Teneridrilus mastrix* (*)	China	California	1984
	Polychaeta	*Desdemona ornata* (*)	South Africa, Australia	Italy	1986
		Marenzelleria viridis	U.S. Atlantic	Germany	1983
Crustacea	Cladócera	*Bythotrephes cederstroemi*	Europe	Great Lakes	1984
	Mysidacea	*Rhopalophthalmus tattersallae* (*)	Indian Ocean	Kuwait	1981
		Neomysis japonica	Japan	Australia	1977
		Neomysis americana (*)	U.S. Atlantic	Argentina, Uruguay	1979
	Cumacea	*Nippoleucon hinumensis*	Japan	California	1980?
				Oregon	1979
	Copepoda	*Pseudodiaptomus inopinus*	Asia	Columbia River	1990
		Pseudodiaptomus marinus	Japan	California	1986
		Pseudodiaptomus forbesi	China	California	1987
		Sinocalanus doerrii	China	California	1978
		Oithona davisae	Asia	California	1979
				Chile	1983
		Limnoithona sinensis	China	California	1979
		Centropages abdominalis	Japan	Chile	1983
		Centropages typicus	U.S. Atlantic	Texas	1985
		Acartia omorii	Japan	Chile	1983
	Decapoda: Brachyura	*Hemigrapsus sanguineus*	Asia	New Jersey	1988
		Charybdis helleri	Indo-Pacific, Israel	Colombia (Caribbean)	1987
	Decapoda: Caridea	*Salmoneus gracilipes* (*)	Japan, Micronesia	California	1986
		Hippolyte zostericola (*)	Western Atlantic	Colombia (Atlantic)	1984
		Exopalaemon styliferus (*)	Indonesia, India	Iraq, Kuwait	1983

Mollusca	Gastropoda	*Tritonia plebeia*	Europe	Massachusetts	1983
	Bivalvia	*Potamocorbula amurensis*	Asia	California	1986
		Dreissena polymorpha	Eurasia	Great Lakes	1988
		Dreissena sp.	Eurasia	Great Lakes	1990
		Rangia cuneata (*)	Southern U.S.	New York	1991
		Theora fragilis	Asia	California	1982
		Musculista senhousia (†)	Japan	New Zealand	1980
				Australia	1982
		Ensis americanus	U.S. Atlantic	Germany	1979
Ectoprocta		*Membranipora membranacea* (*)	Europe	New Hampshire, Maine	1987
Pisces		*Gymnocephalus cernuus*	Europe	Great Lakes	1987
		Proterorhinus marmoratus	Black Sea	Great Lakes	1990
		Neogobious melanostomus	Mediterranean	Great Lakes	1990
		Butis koilomatadon	Indo-West Pacific	Nigeria, Cameroon	1983
				Panama Canal	1972
		Rhinogobius brunneus	Japan	Persian Gulf	1987
		Mugiligobius sp.	Taiwan, Philippines	Hawaii	1987
		Sparidentex hasta	Arabian Sea	Australia	1985
		Parablennius thysanius	Philippines, Indian Ocean	Hawaii	1971

* Suggested herein as a ballast-mediated invasion.
† An alternative means of dispersal includes transport as external fouling on ships' hulls. Here we suggest that transport as ephyrae (for Scyphozoa) and hydromedusae (for Hydrozoa) are as probable as transport as fouling polyps.

materials in dredged spoils. However, with conventional wisdom the concerns can be addressed before the sediments are moved. For example, the Crystal Mountain Workshop (NOAA, 1979) considered the problem of cadmium in dredged materials and the consequential transfer to humans through the consumption of shellfish such as clams and oysters, known concentrators of the metal. In the worst possible scenario, oysters living in the spoil region could accumulate cadmium to levels higher than deemed acceptable for consumption by the US Food and Drug Administration. On the other hand, the dredged materials can in certain circumstances be considered a resource for use as construction aggregate, sanitary landfill, beach replenishment and the creation or enhancement of wetlands.

Increased maritime traffic as a consequence of commercial shipping can interfere with the passenger vessels so important to tourism (Grenon and Batisse, 1989). Already some 60 accidents involving vessels at sea occur annually and in principle this figure will increase with the expected rise in the number of vessels. However, improved navigational facilities and monitoring activities can substantially reduce this number.

Perhaps the most ecologically damaging impact of ship movements is the transport of organisms in ballast waters. The biota from the area in which the water are taken can often survive the journey to the discharge site, especially where temperature and salinity differences are small. Carlton and Geller (1993) have examined the waters from 159 Japanese ships which sailed from 25 ports to Coos Bay, Oregon. There were representatives of all marine trophic groups.

These authors have documented recent invasion of organisms from one country to another (Table 5.4). Some of the invasions can be catastrophic – for example, of zebra mussels into the Laurentian Great Lake, the Asian clam into San Francisco Bay and the comb jelly into the Black Sea.

Another concern involves the transportation of toxic organisms from one port to another in the ballast water of ships. Of 80 cargo vessels entering Australian ports, 6 were found to contain cysts of the toxic dinoflagellates *Alexandrium cutinella* and *A. tamarense* (Hallegraff, G. M. and Bolch, C. J., 1991) Blooms of these organisms are occurring in places that had not been identified previously.

Measures to minimize the import of toxic organisms clearly must be implemented by local authorities. These might include (1) certification that, at the ports visited, the waters were free of toxic organisms; (2) proof of reballasting at sea; (3) treatment of ballast waters to remove toxic organisms; (4) discharge of ballast waters in designated safe areas; (5) mechanisms to keep sediments containing the organisms out of the ballast tanks; and (6) prohibition of the discharge of ballast waters in the port of entry (Hallegraff and Bolch, *op. cit.*).

Undersea tunnels

The concept of undersea tunnels is centuries old. Today, they have been constructed over distances of 50 km or greater. The longest one, Seikan Undersea Tunnel, connects Honshu with Hokkaido, Japan, and is 53.85 km in length (Mochida, 1990). The English Channel has been spanned with a tunnel of 52.5 km length and depths of 100 m (Guterl and Ruthen, 1991). The Japanese are perhaps the most productive in this area with the Kanmon Undersea Tunnel (3.6 km) and the New Kammon Undersea Tunnel for the Shinkansen bullet train connecting Honshu and Kyushi (Mochida, 1990). Construction is planned of the Honyo Strait Tunnel (40 km) linking Shikoku and Kyushu.

The construction of undersea tunnels are veritable feats of civil engineering. The English Channel tunnel (nicknamed the 'Chunnel') involved 14,000 workers and the removal of several million metric tons of sediment.

The high costs of construction will clearly limit undersea tunnel development. For very short distances, bridges may be more rational; for longer distances, the ferry is the economically favoured means of transportation. The use of electrically propelled trains for the long tunnels eliminates the problem of exhaust gases from combustion-driven vehicles, but, there is the significant problem in the movement of air within the tunnel over long distances.

The conflict of undersea tunnels with other users of coastal space will involve primarily the land areas needed for entry and exit spaces.

The information gained in the construction of the tunnels can be applied to other anticipated uses of undersea space: industrial plants, habitation and storage. Clearly, the vertical dimension of coastal zone space will increase in importance with time.

References

Aquat. Rep. Monitoring and surveillance of non-radioactive contaminants in the aquatic environment and activities regulating the disposal of waste at sea. Aquat. Environmental Monitoring Report 6, Lowestoft, United Kingdom. 48 p. (1993).

Brown, L. R. and Young, J. E. Growing food in a warmer world. *World Water* 1, 31–6 (1988).

Carleton, J. T. and Geller, J. B. Ecological roulette: the global transport of non-indigenous marine organisms. *Science* 261, 78 (1993).

Grenon, M. and Batisse, M. *Futures for the Mediterranean Basin. The Blue Plan.* Oxford University Press. xviii + 279 p. (1989).

Guerl, F. and Ruthen, R. Chunnel vision. *Sci. American* 246, 22–8 (1991).

Hallegraff, G. M. and Bolch, C. J. Transport of toxic dinoflagellate cysts via ship ballast water. *Mar. Poll. Bull.* 22, 27–30 (1991).

Mochida, Y. Construction of a space in the seabed. In: *The Oceans in Human Affairs,* ed. S. Fred Singer. Paragon House, New York. pp. 281–94 (1990).

NAS. *Dredging Coastal Ports.* National Academy Press. Washington, D.C., 212 p. (1985a).

NAS. *Oil in the Sea.* National Academy Press. Washington, D.C. 601 p. (1985b).

NOAA. Assimilative Capacity of US Coastal Waters for Pollutants. US National Ocean and Atmospheric Administration. Environmental Research Laboratories, Boulder, Colorado. 284 p. (1979).

6. Energy from the sea

The continuous recovery of energy from the sea remains elusive, although it is often featured in national magazines and Sunday supplements to newspapers. The economics of the construction of the appropriate structures are formidable. Still, advocates of various possible systems remain unperturbed. They are especially encouraged by the argument that the three promising technologies, ocean thermal, tidal and wave energy conversions, do not contribute greenhouse gases to the environment.

Introduction

Recovering energy from the sea is a longtime dream of marine scientists. Today several technologies look attractive: ocean thermal energy conversion (OTEC), tidal energy conversion and wave energy conversion. The schemes have been the foci of many international meetings, books and articles; yet they remain, to a large extent, unfulfilled expectations. All require high capital investments. Nevertheless, there is the hope in the minds of many that engineering advances or social needs will bring them into being in the near future.

OTEC

The most notorious of the schemes is OTEC, which utilizes the temperature difference between warm surface and cold deep waters to run a turbine in a closed or open cycle (Figs. 6.1 and 6.2). Seawater or other substances such as ammonia are used as the working fluid. Warm fluids under high pressure expand to run the turbine and are condensed by cold deep seawater. The turbine generates electricity. The required temperature difference is 17°C or greater (Cohen, 1982). Optionally, where seawater is used as the working fluid, the condensate can be returned to the oceans or collected as a by-product – freshwater – in an open-cycle apparatus (Fig. 6.2). The geographic zone in which OTEC is plausible centres on the equator and extends to the north and to the south by 20° of latitude. It is noteworthy that only three developed nations are within the belt: United States, Japan and Australia.

The electrical energy generated can be used directly or for the production of chemicals such as ammonia, hydrogen or methanol (Craven, 1982). By-products of OTEC operations include nutrient-rich deep seawater, which in principle can be used to fertilize marine plants, the basis of the food chain and potential food for higher organisms.

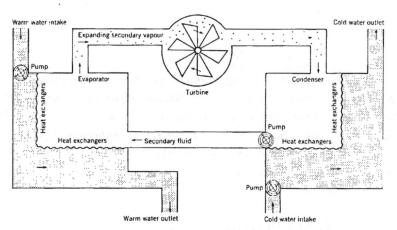

Figure 6.1. Schematic representation of an OTEC closed-cycle system (Cohen, 1982)

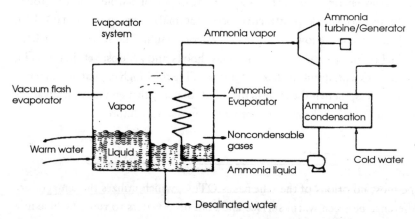

Figure 6.2. Schematic for Hybrid Cycle (HC)-OTEC (Rogers et al., 1988)

The theoretical thermodynamic efficiencies of OTEC are about 7 per cent, but the net efficiencies that can actually be obtained are closer to 2.7 per cent. This difference results from temperature gradients across the heat exchangers and the energies needed to circulate the water (Cohen, 1982). This low efficiency is compensated by a zero cost for the fuel.

Two schemes have been proposed for recovery of energy using this system. One involves the use of an island whose sloping seafloor provides a rest for the pipe carrying the cold water. The second involves a shipboard operation. The number of proposed plants far outnumber those that have been brought to activity (Vadus and Takahashi, 1991) (Table 6.1).

The feasability of OTEC was shown in 1979 with a pilot floating plant, Mini-Otec, built by the Lockheed Corporation, Alfa Laval, the Dillingham Corporation, Worthington Pump, Roto Flow and the State of Hawaii. It was a closed cycle operation. A 60 cm diameter pipe brought cold water to the surface from a depth of 650 m. More than 10 kilowatts of net power were produced (Craven, 1982).

In 1980 a floating test facility was built onboard a World War-II tanker about 30 km off the Kona coast in Hawaii (Cohen, 1982). The plant was used to evaluate heat transfer processes, biofouling and countermeasures, and corrosion. A cold water pipe of 2 m went to a depth of 700 m. Although only limited performance data were produced in the five months of operation, the tests were as successful in rough as in calm waters. Continued efforts are being made to construct additional pilot plants (Rogers et al., 1988). In the State of Hawaii a non-profit corporation, the Pacific International Center for High Technology Research, has been formed in conjunction with the Energy and

Table 6.1. OTEC development projects
(from Vadus and Takahashi, 1991)

Country	Location	Year	Size (kW)	Type of cycle	Comments
USA	Hawaii	1979	50	Closed	Mini-OTEC (built & tested)
USA	Hawaii	1981	1,000	Closed	OTEC-1(thermal exch test only)
USA/UK/Can	Hawaii	1991	180	Closed	Planned
USA	Hawaii	1993	165	Open	Experimental (DOE)
Japan	Naura	1981	100	Closed	Built & tested
Japan	Kyushu	1982	25	Closed	Built & tested
Japan	Tokunoshima	1982	50	Closed	Built & tested
Japan	Univ. of Saga	1985	75	Closed	Thermal exch test only

Resources Division of the US Department of Energy to build a hybrid reactor in which warm seawater, converted to steam, is used to evaporate a working fluid, either ammonia or freon.

Maricultural activities using the high nutrient containing deep waters, the production of fresh water and, refrigeration with the deep waters, are incorporated into the pilot project. Rogers *et al.* (*op. cit.*) argue that the cold waters can be used to cool a 300-room hotel from a megawatt plant with trivial effects upon electrical production.

The initial pilot plant of around 165 kW will be built on a Pacific Island with the goal of eventually producing commercial plants of 1-10 megawatt capacity. The forty-inch diameter cold water pipe is to be 6000 feet in length. The plant will be capable of pumping 13,000 gallons per minute from a depth of 2200 feet.

Whether or not OTEC becomes a commercial reality before the turn of the twentieth century remains to be seen. Demands for low-cost energy in the face of rising fossil fuel costs can set the stage for further engineering tests. A basic requirement remains the construction of a successful prototype in the range of 1–50 megawatts.

OTEC advocates are enthusiastic. Craven (1982) states 'OTEC could contribute to the needs of the entire Pacific Basin before the turn of the century and be a major source of world energy in the first decade of the twentieth century'. Up to now most of the activity has been focused towards the Pacific Islands where energy needs are relatively small. Thus, if OTEC is to be developed there, the produced energy must be exportable, i.e. in the form of fertilizers, aluminium, etc.

Tidal energy

Energy can be drawn from the gravitational forces exerted by the Moon and the Sun upon the Earth – the production of ocean tides. The simplest way to harness tidal energy involves placing a barrier with sluices and turbines across a marine basin (Bruce, 1985). At high tide, the sluices are open and filling of the basin takes place. They are then closed. As the tide falls the sluices are opened, and the outflowing water drives the turbines. By using two basins, one which fills the other, and by employing differing drainage periods, electricity from the turbines can be generated nearly continuously. With only one basin, energy is generated primarily during ebb tide. A tidal range of five metres is necessary for the production of electricity. The high tidal ranges in the Bay of Funday in Canada and the Severn Estuary in the United Kingdom make them especially attractive for tidal energy generation. In the former case, enthusiasm has diminished as excessive fish kills are predicted and tidal changes as far south as Boston might come about (Patton, 1991). The appropriate coupling of tidal forces with basin geometry limits power generation to latitudes 50–60°.

Bruce (1985) indicates that a successful tidal energy plant is operating at the mouth of the river Rance in Brittany, France. It was completed in 1967 with an output of 240 MW and has been in successful operation since then, with the turbines apparently showing little wear. Smaller plants have been built in China, Canada and the Soviet Union (Table 6.2). He further points out that there are probably only 30 sites that can usefully be employed for tidal energy recovery and that the size of the plants will be comparable to those of the largest hydroelectric power stations. For example, it is argued that the Severn Estuary site could host a plant producing 10 per cent of the annual needs in electrical energy of the United Kingdom.

Table 6.2. Major tidal power developments (Vadus and Takahashi, 1991)

Country	Location	Mean Tide range (m)	Output (MW)	Initial operation
China	Shashan	5.1	0.04	1959
France	La Rance	8.5	240.0	1966
USSR	Kislayan Gulf	3.9	0.4	1968
China	Jingang Creek	5.1	0.165	1970
China	Yuepu		0.15	1971
China	Ganzhutan		5.0	1974
China	Liuhe		0.15	1975
China	Beisakou		0.96	1978
China	Jiangxia Creek	5.1	3.2	1980
Japan	Kurushima		0.002	1983
Canada	Annapolis Royal	7.1	19.1	1984
China	Xingfuyang	5.1	1.28	1989

Wave energy

There have been many ideas on how to harness the kinetic energy of waves but today most converge around devices which compress air that is used to run a turbine connected to a generator (NAS, 1990). Although deeper offshore waters can, in principle, provide more energy, the engineering difficulties in anchoring a large structure capable of withstanding incoming waves appear to limit the location of the plant. There is also the problem of energy transmission to shore.

The simplest device, the oscillating water column (OWC) turbine, has a large chamber in communication with the sea. The turbine outlet is small

Table 6.3. Major wave energy experiments
(Vadus and Takahashi, 1991)

Country	Location	Wave power (kW/m)	Technology	Rating (kW)	Comments
Norway	Toftestallen	7.0	Multiresonant OWC	500	Operated (85–89)
Norway	Toftestallen	7.0	Tapered channel	350	Operating (86)
Norway	Java	20–25	Tapered channel	1,500	Operation (92)
Norway	Tasmania	30–32	Tapered channel	1,500	Operation (92)
Denmark	Hanstholm	9.0	Heaving buoy	45	Tested 1990
UK	Islay	5–15	Shore-based OWC	75	Operation (91)
UK (inactive)	Mauritius		Shore-based OWC	500	Proposed
India (UK) (inactive)	Madras		Offshore OWC	5,000	Proposed
India	Southwest Coast		Offshore caisson OWC	150	Pending
Japan	Yura		KAIMEL, Barge-mounted OWC	125	Operated (78–80 and 85-86)
Japan	Sanze		Shore-based OWC	40	Operated (83–84)
Japan	Sakata Port		Breakwater OWC	60	Operating (89)
Japan	Kujukuri		Shore-based OWC	30	Operating (88)
Japan	Mashike		Breakwater pivoting flap	20	Operating (83)
Sweden	Gottenberg		Heaving buoy	30	Tested 1989
Spain (Sweden)	Atlantic Coast		Heaving buoy	1,000	Proposed (inactive)
Portugal	Azores		Shore-based OWC	300	Proposed
USSR	Makhachkala		Heaving buoy	50	Tested
China	Dawan Island		Shore-based OWC	8	Constructing
USA	Puerto Rico		Heaving buoy	350	
			Desalination project (GPD)		Operating (89)

OWC = Oscillating Water Column

compared to the chamber which causes a speed-up in the air motion. Valves control the operation on the intake and exhaust strokes.

Japan and Norway appear to be at the forefront of wave energy activity, with the United Kingdom not far behind (Duckers, 1989; Vadus and Takahashi, 1991; Table 6.3). The Asian country constructed a shore-fixed 40 kW OWC at Sanze, Tauruoaka City, on the northwest coast of Japan. The overall efficiency for the conversion of wave energy to electricity was 0.11 in tests conducted in 1983. A second Japanese device, Kaimei, is contained on a moored vessel with a collection of 13 OWCs. It was tested during the 1970s and 1980s and had an average efficiency of 0.065.

The Norwegians have constructed two prototype wave power stations north of Bergen. The 600-kW OWC operated successfully from January 1987 to early winter in 1988 when it was lost to a storm with wave heights of 11 m. Two 500-kW OTCs were planned for the forthcoming year.

References

Bruce, M. Ocean Energy: Some perspectives on economic viability. In: *Ocean Yearbook 5*, ed. E. M. Borgese and Norton Ginsberg. University of Chicago Press. pp. 58–78 (1985).

Cohen, R. Energy from the Ocean. *Phil. Trans. R. Soc.* London 307A, 405–37 (1982).

Craven, John P. *The Management of Pacific Marine Resources: Present Problems and Future Trends.* Westview Press, Boulder, Colorado. xix + 105 p. (1982).

Duckers, L. J. (ed.). *Wave Energy Devices.* The Solar Energy Society Proceedings. Coventry, United Kingdom. 30 Nov. 1989. 80 p. (1989).

NAS. *Our Seabed Frontier.* National Academy Press. Washington D.C. xvii + 138 p. (1990).

Patton, Donald J. Canadian policies and programs for coastal ocean space utilization. Second International Symposium on Coastal Ocean Space Utilization. 2–4 April, 1991. Long Beach, California, USA (1991).

Rogers, L. J., Matsuda, F., Vega, L. and Takahashi, P. K. (1988). Converting ocean thermal energy for commercial use in the Pacific. *Sea Technology* 29 (10), 23–29 (1988).

Vadus, J. R. and Takahashi, P. K. The potential of ocean energy conversion systems for island and coastal applications. Manuscript presented to the Second International Symposium on Coastal Ocean Space Utilization, 2–4 April 1991, Long Beach, California, USA (1991.

7. Commercial fishing

Although the commercial catch of fish has somewhat stabilized at 100 million tons per year, changes in fishing techniques have decreased the need for coastal zone space substantially.

Introduction

The need for US coastal zone space by the commercial fishing industry has been decreasing over the past years. Although the demand for marine food products has been rising, a number of factors combine to lessen the requirements for support facilities in harbour areas. (Fricke, 1991; many of the concepts in this chapter derive from this presentation). First of all, there have been changes in fishing technique – the small fishing boats have been displaced by larger vessels, the catcher/processors, which require different types of port space. Secondly, maricultured products are competing successfully with the products from the wild and they are increasing annually. Also, recreational uses of coastal zone space are economically more rewarding than those of the fisheries. Finally, the potential of existing fisheries is being diminished by the physical alterations of estuaries and wetlands which can diminish areas of the breeding and nursery grounds of some commercial fisheries.

The shift from fishing to recreational pursuits

Space for wharves, boat yards and related industrial activities, crucial parts of the small boat fishing activity, have been pre-empted for habitat, marinas, yacht clubs, restaurants and hotels/motels. Economically, the land areas are much more attractive for recreational and living space.

An example of these changes is found in the small harbours and bays of Southern California (Johnson and Metzger, 1983). Over the last half of the twentieth century the commercial uses of the coastal zone, once involved with wharves and fish landings, commercial boat yards and related marine activities, have shifted to recreational services (tour boats, sports fishing boats, boat charters and rentals) recreational activities (boating, fishing, swimming, skin diving, sun bathing) and ancillary needs (recreational boat yards, brokerages, dive shops, restaurants, hostelries, among others). Johnson and Metzger (1983) call this a shift from 'technical to expressive interests'. Leisure replaced work as the coastal zone activity.

Newport Beach exemplifies the changes that took place between Santa Barbara and San Diego, California (Johnson and Metzger, 1983). Following dredging of Newport Bay at the turn of the century, a fishing fleet and processing plants evolved. By the second decade of the twentieth century, pleasure pursuits entered with day boats, yacht clubs and other devices of leisure. Following World War II, the shipbuilding came to an end and the fishing vessels moved southward and northward to San Diego and San Pedro respectively. By the beginning of the last decade of the twentieth century, there are but a few fishing boats left.

As economic factors have driven the technical enterprises out of the harbour, today even some of the recreational users are being affected by rising costs, space and labour. The high costs of suitable sites for boatbuilding have been such that many enterprises have relocated to Florida or the east coast sites which enjoy lower real estate values (Johnson and Metzger, 1983).

Fisheries space

The Magnuson Fishery Conservation and Management Act passed by Congress in 1976 provided the springboard for the increased role of the United States in commercial fisheries in the Exclusive Economic Zone (EEZ). The demand for marine food products has also risen. Fricke (*op. cit.*) notes the consequential rise in the number of commercial fishermen from 173,610 to 273,700 persons between 1976 and 1988, with a corresponding increase in the number of large vessels, factory-trawlers and other catcher/processing vessels. During this period smaller boats declined by 19 per cent to 69,600 in 1988 while larger vessels increased by 40 per cent to 23,300. However, overall, the total number of commercial fishing craft declined from 102,621 to 92,900.

Catcher/processors, whose average length is 231 feet, operate off all US coasts, but primarily in Alaska, and deliver today 2,336,000 metric tons annually, while the smaller groundfish trawlers, with an average length of 82 feet, produce 635,700 metric tons.

Environmental change

The fishermen in the wild have been displaced from the coastal zone as competition for space has increased, stock abundances have decreased (in part due to overfishing and in part due to loss of estuarine and wetland areas, the nursery and breeding ground for much of their catch), and the trawler/processor has taken over.

Mariculture

The impact of mariculture upon the coastal and open ocean fisheries has been discussed previously. Perhaps both will rise together in absolute terms for the future. For the next years, mariculture will clearly increase at the more rapid rate.

References

Fricke, P. H. Multiple Use Compatibility: Commercial fishing and coastal zone development. Manuscript presented to the Second International Symposium on Coastal Ocean Space Utilization. 2–4 April, 1991. Long Beach, California, USA (1991).

Johnson, J. C. and Metzger, D. The shift from technical to expressive use of small harbors: The 'Play-Full' harbors of southern California. *Coastal Zone Management Journal* 10, 429–41 (1983).

8.   Offshore minerals

Offshore recovery of minerals, primarily those containing magnesium, potassium and bromium, have reduced the quality of the coastal environs. As demands for aggregate, shells and placer materials mount, environmental protection policies will be necessary.

Introduction

Of the minerals extracted from the marine environment, aggregates which include sands, gravels and shells, are economically third in importance following hydrocarbons and sulphur and the salts of seawater from which NaCl, Mg and Br are obtained (Table 8.1). The granulates are used in the production of concrete, beach replenishment, roadfill and landfill, and the construction of artificial islands. In addition, there are the placer minerals which have been beneficiated and include gold, titanium oxides, phosphates and chromites.

Table 8.1. *Value (in US dollars) of minerals extracted from the marine environment (Charlier and Charlier, 1991)*

Minerals	1960	1967	1980
Sand and gravel, including rock, limestone, felspars	47	60	6000 (est.)
Mg, NaCl, Br	69	85	—
Hydrocarbons and sulphur	433	1405	—

Sand and gravel

Today, the largest exploitation of sand and gravel from coastal waters takes place in Japan and the United Kingdom with only modest changes over the past decade (Charlier and Charlier, 1992; Table 8.2). About one quarter of Japan's needs are extracted from the sea (Table 8.2) while for the United States and the United Kingdom the requirements are much less. The United States reserves are estimated to be 1743 billion tons of sand and 60 billion tons of gravel. About 70 per cent of continental shelves are covered by mineable granulates which accumulated during the Quaternary glaciations (Charlier and Charlier, 1992). The needs of all countries for aggregate are increasing. For example, the Pacific Island countries, including the Cook Islands, the Solomon Islands, Samoa, Fiji, Guam, Tonga, Kiribati, Vanatu and Tuvalu, are likely to make significant demands upon the world aggregate supply (McCloy, 1984). As land resources become more scarce and transportation costs from distant land sites rise, so there will be more dependence upon marine sources.

Both land and sea areas are needed for aggregate operations. Shore space requirements in the United Kingdom for an individual dredger which recovers between 1500 and 2000 tons per day are of the order of one to two acres for unloading, processing and stockpiling (Archer, 1973).

Table 8.2. Sand and gravel production in thousands of tons (Charlier and Charlier, 1992)

Country	Marine production			Total production	
	1978	1982	1990	1982	1990
Japan	84,700		70,000		280,000
United Kingdom	18,000	16,500	16,000		106,600
Denmark	4,600	5,040		40,800	
USA	4,000			595,000	
The Netherlands	2,430				
France	2,800	4,200	2,500	341,000	250,000
Belgium	1,140				
Iceland	600				
Germany (FR)	20				

Gravel deposits are usually found in depths of less than 50 metres where the currents range from 2 to 4 knots. Sands occur where currents have speeds between 1.5 to 2 knots; below these speeds, muds accumulate (Charlier and Charlier, 1992).

There are remarkable regional distributions of marine aggregates. For example, in the United Kingdom, more than 80 per cent of the sites are located in south Wales. The major dredging areas are the Humber, the Thames, the east and south coasts of England, the Bristol Channel, Liverpool Bay and the Mersey River in Wales (Nicholls, 1991). In the United States sands are recovered from the offshore waters in New York and Florida, Mississippi and California while sand and gravel is taken from New Jersey, Connecticut and Texas.

Environmental impacts

The recovery of sand and gravel can interfere with normal erosional processes, the coastal fisheries, and the integrity of submarine cables and oil/gas pipelines, though only the first two appear today to be substantial.

Sand and gravel mining can alter the coastal environment to the disadvantage of indigenous organisms. Fish nursing and breeding grounds can be destroyed or altered in detrimental ways. The increased turbidity can reduce plant productivity and the metabolic activity of animals, and put at risk the food supply for organisms at a higher trophic level. Whole ecosystems can be altered through the removal of sandbanks.

On the other hand, some scientists and engineers argue that where the new sediment surface is identical to the original one, the benthos will quickly reestablish itself and there will be no long-term changes in the contours of the bottom profile.

Drawdown of sedimented material from the shallower zones to deeper dredged areas is clearly possible. Uren (1988) argues that each site must be evaluated individually for such an impact. Clearly, the coastal deposit regime should be kept in a renewable state and dredging prohibited where damage is likely. Especially sensitive areas such as bars and banks which can be eroded by wave attack must be protected.

Sand and gravel resources from the sea compete with their land-based counterparts. Distances from the quarry site to the use site are ever-increasing in developed areas. The relative transport costs of land and sea sand and gravel, coupled with the quality of the material, will determine, to a large extent, which will have the competitive advantage. In some cases the rental of shore space for marine activities may seriously effect the financial picture. Of course, it must be remembered that deeper sites for dredging will come about as the technology advances.

Shell material

Shells, the exoskeletons of marine organisms, are primarily calcium carbonate and can be recovered from the coastal zone for use as chemical intermediates and, like sand and gravel, be used as construction materials. They are usually relict material and are found primarily in the middle and low latitudes (Drucker and Rowland, 1991). Shells have been mined off Iceland for the production of Portland Cement and there are extensive deposits off the northern and western coasts of Scotland (Cronan, 1992).

Placer deposits

Placer deposits arise from the weathering of crustal rocks, igneous, metamorphic and sedimentary, and accumulate in the coastal zone as a result of riverine, eolian and shore transport. The minerals proposed for beneficiation include gold, titanium oxides, cassiterite phosphates, and chromites. About 80 per cent of the global production of rutile, 50 per cent of ilmenite and 30 per cent of the cassiterite are extracted from marine areas (Kudras, 1987). The majority of zircon is mined from the sea.

References

Archer, A. A. Sand and gravel demands on the North Sea – Present and Future. *In: North Sea Science,* ed. E. D. Goldberg, MIT Press, Cambridge, Mass. pp. 436–49 (1973).

Charlier, R. H., and Charlier, C. C. Environmental, economic and social aspects of marine aggregates exploitation. *Environmental Conservation* 18. (1992).

Cronan, David S. *Marine Minerals in Exclusive Economic Zones.* Chapman and Hall, London, viii + 209 p. (1992).

Kudras, H. Sedimentary models to estimate the heavy mineral potential of shelf sediments. *In: Marine Minerals,* ed. P. G. Teleki, M. R. Dobson, J. R. Moore and U. von Stackeborg. D. Reidel, Dordrecht, pp. 39–56 (1987).

Tsurusaki, K., Iwasaki, T. and Arita, M. Seabed sand mining in Japan. *Marine Mining,* 7, 49–67 (1988).

Uren, J. M. The marine sand and gravel dredging industry of the United Kingdom. *Marine Mining,* 7, 69–88 (1988).

Young, J. E. Mining the Earth. *In: State of the World,* ed. L. R. Brown. W. W. Norton & Co., New York, pp. 100–18 (1992).

9. Use conflicts and regulatory mechanisms

Both national and international regulatory policies relating to the management of the coastal zone to a large extent can well be considered in terms of property. The focus of the Law of the Sea Convention has been on issues relating to property over which it had no jurisdiction. On the other hand, national issues can involve public, private and common property. Recent scientific and economic developments, not incorporated into national policies, can make coastal zone conflicts more difficult to resolve.

Introduction

The protection of the users of marine resources, as well as of the general public concerned with misuse, can come about through regulation at various national and international levels. Problems involving one nation impinging upon the coastal resources of another (for example the Po River pollution in the northern Adriatic where the sources are primarily Italian but the impacts are felt to some extent by Crotia and Slovenia, or the poaching of ranched fish managed by members of one nation by citizenry of another nation on the high seas) are beginning to emerge.

The competition for coastal ocean space in some areas is becoming fierce; the protection of that space even fiercer. Regulatory actions will probably be slanted in favour of those activities which are economically advantageous. Thus, touristic and recreational activities may claim the highest priority.

Such appears to be the case in the Mediterranean (World Bank, 1990).

With a near doubling of the coastal population expected by 2025, and with all of the large cities essentially in the coastal zone, it is vital that use of the available area be planned as a whole. A few countries are taking steps to minimize use conflicts. France, Italy and Spain are taking inventories of the existing and potential resources with the aim of bringing about balanced development. For example, 42 per cent of the 8000 km of coastal zone in Spain is, as yet, unoccupied and the new laws and policies have been formulated to minimize unregulated development. The new policies define the coastal strip as public domain with access limited. Similarly, Israel's 190 km coastal region is unoccupied or used for activities that do not need to be in the coastal zone. The increasing demand for expanded recreational activities are directing environmental agencies to prepare regulations for the protection of the resources.

Bowden (1981) has studied the history of regulatory constraints upon mariculture in California. These impediments are numerous and they have hindered the development of sea farming and ranching there. The author concludes that the situation has been caused by:

1. the large number of agencies involved;
2. complex and technical regulations;
3. public policies and laws often in conflict;
4. many regulations that predate the birth of aquaculture; and
5. laws that fail to respond to the users' needs.

Regulations should protect the coastal zone from both overuse and underuse. In the case of overuse, nearly any type of ranching can provide a reasonable example. For instance, if too many small salmon are introduced to the sea, they could deplete sources of food such as anchovies and damage natural food chains. This clearly would be counterproductive to the salmon ranchers. Controls would be essential.

The role of the coastal ocean in the disposal of non-recyclable wastes, even those classified as hazardous, will probably increase in the future. This present example of the underuse of the coastal ocean stems from the oft-times uneconomical and unscientific insistence on land disposal by regulatory agencies and environmental groups.

The coastal ocean, whether it be the land on one side or the water on the other, can be considered as property. Bowden (1981) provides an appropriate entry to the subject with the definition that 'property consists solely of rights and that all rights stem from government'. We shall be guided by Bowden in the following discussion.

He defines the three types of property:

* *private property* encompasses those rights endowed by government to private individuals or groups;

- *public property* encompasses those rights endowed by government to a public agency;
- *common property* encompasses those rights in a natural resource granted by a government and held by a class of users whose rights are co-equal.

Clearly of importance in the coastal zone is the existence of a resource in the definition of property. The sovereign nation must have control over the property to assign rights to the exploitation of a resource. On such a basis, as Bowden points out, ferromanganese minerals in the deep sea or the ozone layer in the atmosphere are not property at all. They are not under the jurisdiction of a sovereign authority, yet minerals contribute an important item on the agenda of the Law of the Sea conferences.

The seas over which governments have control, say the 200-mile zone, are clearly common property. Once fish are caught they become private property. Those parts of the ocean over which governments have no control are not property and clearly liable to free access.

The development of extensive mariculture in a coastal regime may come into conflict with growing transportation and recreational uses. Marine property (rights) thus is in need of identification. Bowden (*op. cit.*) suggests that this might be done in one of three ways. Firstly, we can create private property in the sea as we have done on land. Secondly, public property might be identified: governments would control the resource and sell off parts as they see fit. Finally, common property can be created and the rights of use can be defined for co-equal users.

The control by governments of a common property resource in the end may be most attractive. They can control the use of the resource. More than one company may wish to establish fish farms in a given area. Each could be licensed to use the common waters. Regulations as to the placement of fish pens, the amounts of therapeutants that might be used and the numbers of fish that may be farmed at any one time would be formulated by a relevant government agency. The waste discharges from land would have to be controlled to minimize impacts upon the maricultural activity.

Bowden poses arguments against the common property concept applied to mariculture. First of all, it can impact upon existing ecosystems. The creation of an anoxic seafloor or of nutrient-enriched waters can lead to undesirable effects such as the loss of benthic communities or eutrophication. He is also concerned that the continued advances in maricultural techniques can force commercial fishermen and shell-fishermen out of business through more cost-effective ways of producing their commodities. Also, the general public might not receive a just and equitable return through the grant of the use of common resources. Bowden counters these arguments with the concept that the public indeed will benefit from such developments and there is a price to be paid. He accepts the concern that the seascape may be altered, perhaps in unpleasant ways, by the existence of the fishpens. The increased new employment opportunities, capital gains, new wealth and new food supplies are the compensations.

Maricultural activities will probably increase to the extent that their products will continue to approach both in weight and in monetary value the catches of wild organisms, perhaps up to 20 per cent. Since there is a substantial labour input into ranching and farming, these developments will probably be more intensive in the developing than in the developed world. The former has other growing economic resources that can be seriously threatened by maricultural developments, such as recreational and industrial uses of the coasts. Already we have seen use conflicts in areas such as Hong Kong (see Chapter 4).

Finally, the use of the oceans within the 200-mile exclusive economic zone for waste disposal might preferably be treated as public or private property, i.e. the rights of use are sold or given to public or private institutions. In such a way the local authorities can maintain jurisdiction over the ocean zone through the sale of discharge rights. Much as offshore oil exploration and drilling rights are managed by the Bureau of Land Management in the United States, so offshore dumping rights can be managed by an appropriate agency. Clearly, disposal areas may move from one place to another, in much the same way that as land-based dumps can reach saturation and the activity must be moved to other areas.

Formulation of regulations

Maricultural activities on a large scale are a rather recent development. Further, scientific and engineering interests are growing nearly as rapidly as the field itself. Thus, the enactment of regulations require strong and continuing collaboration between engineers and scientists and those in the political arena of regulation. Regulations are needed not only to protect the general public from misuse of common property but also to protect the farmer himself from damaging activities of other users of ocean space. Yet regulations require enforcement, and the haunting question is 'How many policemen can we afford?'

Recent scientific reports give guidance on regulatory activity in marine farming. For example, restrictions on siting can come about as a result of aesthetic and scientific concerns as well as conflicts with other programmes. For example, the following questions, when answered, can give rise to regulations in a given location:

1. How close to each other can pens of a given size be sited? Clearly, the answer will depend upon the type of fish, the size to which they are grown, etc.

2. What is the level of tidal flushing required to minimize a tendency toward biological misbalance, i.e. oxygen utilization and nutrient generation?

Also, regulations concerning the use of potential biocides are in order. Already, in many states and countries the use of tributyltin as an antifoulant on parts of aquaculture structures is prohibited. Concerns about the levels of therapeutants remaining in product organisms through to consumption and about their impact upon indigenous organisms have been raised. Regulations may offer both the ecosystems and the general public some protection.

The inhibitory effects of laws and regulations can well be seen in the growing shrimp mariculture industry (Rosenberry, 1990). The world shrimp industry currently generates about 3 billion dollars annually (based on a price to the shrimpers of $2.50 per pound). Maricultured shrimp may double its share of the market by the year 2000 to produce 3.3 billion pounds in a 6.6 billion pound market.

At the present time the eastern hemisphere far outranks the western hemisphere in production (Table 9.1). China controls essentially 30 per cent of the output. Can the West effectively compete with the East? There are many attractive areas for shrimp mariculture. Rosenberry argues that lack of government support, restrictive regulations, and protectionist policies combine to inhibit involvement by nationals and foreign investors. The countries of the East actively foster shrimp farming. Rosenberry points out that the most prosperous development period for Ecuador in this respect was during a period of office of a free-market president, coupled with good weather. In Mexico, much of the coastal land belongs to agrarian reform communes who are prohibited by law of disposing from their holdings. Potential investors are not interested in involvements with the owners.

The potential US market makes shrimp farming quite attractive to Latin Americans, but capital is necessary. The present economic and social situation may not be supportive of outside entrepreneurs.

Scientists and bureaucracies

One of the difficulties in maintaining regulations in the context of developments in both natural and social sciences is the maintenance of communication between specialists outside government and the bureaucracies. The root of the problem may be in the bureaucracies which have been described by Professor Kenneth Hare as institutions where no actions are taken for the first time or for the last time – Hare's Law. The characterization applies to most national and international agencies charged with maintaining or improving environmental quality.

*Table 9.1. Production of farmed shrimp in the eastern
and western hemispheres in 1989
From Rosenberry (1990)*

	Eastern				Western		
	Per cent production	Heads-on production [pounds]	Acres in production		Per cent production	Heads-on production [pounds]	Acres in production
China	33	364,000,000	385,000	Ecuador	71	99,000,000	173,000
Indonesia	18	198,000,000	618,000	Honduras	6	8,814,000	11,000
Thailand	18	198,000,000	198,000	Peru	5	6,613,000	9,800
Philippines	10	110,000,000	200,000	Columbia	5	6,613,000	9,800
Vietnam	6	66,000,000	395,000	Mexico	4	5,511,000	6,200
India	5	55,000,000	148,000	United States	2	2,645,000	1,000
Taiwan	4	44,000,000	10,000	Guatemala	2	2,645,000	1,000
Other	6	68,000,000	255,000	Panama	1.6	2,204,000	7,400
				Brazil	1.6	2,204,000	7,400
				Cuba	–	772,000	1,235
				Belize	–	441,000	495
Total	100	1,103,000,000	2,209,000	Total	100	138,530,000	233,944

Historically, the regulatory agencies started out with well-defined and achievable goals and strategies, yet they often evolved into sterile, regressive organizations. The problems relating to the pollution of the oceans well support Hare's Law. Instead of carrying out environmental surveillance in critical and cost-effective ways, they repeat, year after year, routine activities that bear little relationship to potential and serious problems.

The measurement of polychlorinated biphenyls (PCBs) in samples from the marine environment provides a useful 'example'. These industrial chemicals, widely used in the past, bear similar toxicities to those of the halogenated hydrocarbon pesticides such as DDT and dieldrin. Yet only ten or so of the 200 congeners (components of the industrial products), the so-called co-planar molecules, can seriously impact upon marine organisms. Measurement of this small group does not take place in any present-day marine monitoring programme allegedly because the cost of the analyses and the associated equipment is high. Yet measurements of total PCB are carried out, which may or may not bear a relationship to the congeners.

The tributyltin problem, discussed in Chapter 2, is regulated in some countries but not in all. Pleasure boats in one country, where regulations exist, are often taken to another where they do not, to have their boats painted with this terribly toxic substance. Also, tributyltin is being substituted with triphenyltin, equally toxic, for which regulations have not been introduced. Most national regulatory agencies have yet to deal with these problems.

Other important potential problems are not addressed, or only weakly so, such as the continuing degradation of coastal waters as evidenced by the increasing frequency of red tides and by massive plankton blooms. Are we in danger of losing any commercial food products from the sea as a consequence of changes in the nature of the plant life? Are other touristic regions in danger of losing recreational areas, as happened in the northern Adriatic?

Is there a solution to these dilemmas? I think there is. Regulatory agencies in many countries have lost regular contact with practising scientists. Developments continually take place in the social and natural sciences and engineering which alter existing concepts, and such information needs to be rapidly transferred to the regulatory community. In many cases this is simply not done.

What is needed is the establishment of substantial advisory committees made up of currently active members of the professions involved with environmental problems. In most agencies such committees do not exist. They could guide the agencies as to what measurements can be done away with, what new measurements and what frequencies of measurement are ideal. In this way pollution problems can be adequately addressed. Similarly, such advisory groups are vital for other areas of coastal zone management. Violations of Hare's Law can then come about.

Environmental impact statements

One of the effective ways of bringing an awareness of potential impacts upon the coastal zone through its exclusive use by an individual or organization is the preparation of an environmental impact statement by the user. UNEP-1990 defines an environmental impact assessment (EIA) as 'the process of identifying, predicting, interpreting and communicating the potential impacts that a proposed project or plan may have on the environment'. Such statements, often considered in multi-volume documents, are extremely important for the decision-making process and, when carefully done, can lead to effective policy and regulations. Monitoring is an essential part of the EIA. With the data, the initial information and predictions can be amended on an on-going basis.

Such documents usually include a detailed description of the activity or project and the parts of the environment which it is likely to affect. The reasons for the site selection, the potential impacts upon public health, ecosystems and the environment itself, the strategies to minimize impacts and the proposed monitoring programme are to be spelled out (UNEP, 1990).

Under some circumstances environmental impact statements may be presented to the general public for their consideration and evaluation. In doing so, the fears and concerns of the citizens can be alleviated, although a more significant aspect to the process is the introspection engendered in the originating individuals and organizations.

Regulating the safety of seafoods

A crucial question relating to the safety of seafood consumption from a given area involves the criteria for monitoring the products. Can we ascertain whether or not pollution associated agents are making seafoods unsafe to eat? The answer is no for several reasons. There is not a single indicator organism for the determination of public health risk in either waters or seafood. In the United States, the only seafoods that are regulated by microbial standards are molluscan shellfish, with an upper limit of fourteen most probable number (MPN) of faecal coliforms per 100 ml of water and with not more than 10 per cent exceeding 43 MPN (FDA, 1989). This criterion is based upon the consumption of raw shellfish from studies made in the 1920s relating the number of *Salmonella typhi* present during typhoid fever epidemics and has been modified subsequently to the present number.

But there are many inadequacies to this standard. First of all, non-faecal pathogens can predominate in any population. Also, non-sewage related naturally occurring bacteria, such as the Vibrionaceae are overlooked. Finally, the faecal coliform indicator does not relate to the presence of enteric viruses such as Norwalk types or Enteroviruses. Clearly, one of the most important steps forward would be the development of indicators for contamination of waters by pathogens of human origin.

There are other factors related to the toxicity of seafoods. Distributional problems mean that products are exposed over time to higher temperatures, allowing microbial populations to grow. Imported seafoods are often from countries with much higher incidents of enteric disease. The import of molluscan seafoods should be prohibited for raw consumption, unless standards for harvest are equal to, or are higher than, those of the importing country (Ahmed, 1991).

Pollutant export

The population increases throughout the planet will be accompanied by steadily-rising fluxes of materials to the coastal ocean by the atmosphere, rivers, outfalls and boat and ship discharges. The awareness of transboundary pollution, i.e. the situation in which the inputs of one country can adversely affect the resources of an adjacent country, require that accurate and continuing records of inputs to the coastal ocean be maintained by sovereign states. These records should be available to other nations to assist them in maintaining the quality of their coastal environment.

An unusual manifestation of the coupling of physical factors and the increased inputs of nutrients to the northern Adriatic led to eutrophication and the loss of touristic revenues in the coastal areas of Yugoslavia and Italy (Vukadin, 1991). The Italian rivers are the source of most of the anthropogenic nutrients (Table 9.2) and have a combined drainage area of 120,000 km², populated by 25 million people constituting half of the Italian population (Amato *et al.*, 1989). The areas impacted by the devastating plankton blooms include the Emilia-Romagna coast and the Lagoon of Venice in Italy and the town port of Pula and Kastela Bay in former Yugoslavia.

Table 9.2. Nutrient loads of rivers entering the north Adriatic (Vukadin, 1991).

River	P salts	N salts
	($\times 10^3$ m³ y⁻¹)	
Po	16.4	114
Rivers south of the Po (Italian)	4.4	37.9
Rivers north of the Po (Italian)	8.6	70.0
Yugoslavian rivers and industry	1.4	8.9

The massive algal blooms have been known since 1972 when the first description of 'dirty water' was described for the Gulf of Venice (Viviani, 1988). Since that time, there have been other similar episodes with anoxia, fish kills and the formation of gelatinous material.

The issues of revenue loss and aesthetic insults create a most sensitive situation. The touristic industry on both sides of the Adriatic amounts to $US 8 billion. Italy ranks as the fifth industrial nation in the world (Pravdic, 1991) and the impacted region receives domestic and industrial wastes from 60 per cent of its population. The ratio of the GNPs of Italy and former Yugoslavia was a factor of five. The development of long-term plans will be needed to alleviate this unacceptable situation.

Additional conflicts

Up to now we have considered those activities involved in coastal zone space utilization that have permanent structures – waste disposal outfalls, harbour facilities for deep-water ports, tourist hotels, mariculture pens, among others.

However, there are other activities that do not require space that is occupied over long time periods – mining operations for sand, gravel, oil, gas, and ores; and fishing. Yet such enterprises can contribute, in one way or another, to a decrease in environmental quality and can conflict with the renewable uses of the coastal zone. The fishing activities in a way differ from those of mining: the former are renewable in principle; the latter are not.

The control of these transient activities requires environmental impact assessments and regulations in a similar way to those for the geographically constrained activities.

References

Amato, F., Chiaudani, G., Giani, M., Pagnotta, R., Pierantonelli, L. and Marchetti, R. Condizioni al contorno. *In: L'Eutrofizzazione nel Mare Adriatico*, ed. P. V. Curzi and F. Tombolini. Proc. Convegno Nazionale 'Per la Difesa dell'Adriatico', Ancona, Italy, pp. 100–9 (1989).

Bowden, G. *Coastal Aquaculture Law and Policy: A Case Study of California*. Westview Press. Boulder, Colorado. xiv + 241 p. (1981).

Pravdic, V. Conceptual framework of environmental management strategies for Yugoslavia. The case of the Adriatic Sea. *Mar. Poll. Bull.* 23 587–604 (1991).

Rosenberry, Bob. World Shrimp Farming. Can the western hemisphere compete with the eastern? *Aqua. Mag.* 18, 60–4 (1990).

UNEP-1990. An approach to environmental impact assessment for projects affecting the coastal and marine environment. UNEP Regional Seas Reports and Studies No. 122. iii + 25 p. (1990).

Viviani, R. Effects of chemical pollutants and phytoplankton bloom on the marine biological resources of the Adriatic Sea. *Ann. New York Acad. Sci.* 534, 986–99 (1988).

Vukadin, I. Impacts of nutrient enrichment and their relation to the algal bloom in the Adriatic Sea. *Mar. Poll. Bull.* 23, 145–8 (1991).

World Bank. *The Environmental Program for the Mediterranean. Preserving a shared heritage and managing a common resource*. World Bank, Washington D.C. ix + 93 p. (1990).

10. Prelude to conflict

The key to minimizing conflicts in the coastal zone is population management.

Introduction

Throughout the world, the pressures for the additional use of coastal zone space will primarily come from the groups involved with tourism and recreation, economically the most important activities. The land and sea areas are essentially fixed in size but the population seeking to live and work there is continuously increasing. Conflicts will inevitably arise among users and potential users, unless appropriate blueprints are formulated for population control and for space utilization in the coastal zone.

Both migration and increasing birth rates (and decreasing death rates) are critical factors determining populations. The migration of people to the coastal zone of one country from another country usually relates to an anticipated better life quality – housing, employment, medical services, educational opportunities, and recreation. Because the coastal zone in general offers a higher quality of life and is more easily accessible than inland areas, it attracts migrants. Today there are movements of peoples from North African countries across the Mediterranean to Spain, Italy and France; from South and Central Americas to the east, gulf and west coasts of the United States, and from northern to southern Brazilian coasts.

The two most important questions for countries receiving immigrants are: how does its citizenry wish to utilize the coastal zone space; and what is the population capacity for such a usage? In any event the population demands will most probably be higher than can be accommodated by the existing space. Further, the population capacity clearly will depend upon what the plans for future development will be.

Clearly, the need for population movement from coastal areas impacted by migration is crucial. Measures to forward this goal can be carried out with broad popular support. In principle, an overcrowding can be mitigated by providing a nearby alternate habitat for the migrants with employment possibilities and the necessary amenities of pleasant living. Such centres of growth could induce alternate paths of migration once they were established. The initial development in general must be subsidized – the formation of appropriate industries and support facilities for the migrating populace. Thus, the plan to protect the existing coastal zone needs to be prepared years in advance. Stimulating population growth can be accomplished by the establishment of universities, industrial centres, medical centres, or agricultural activities. The lure of employment coupled with a reasonable living standard could promote migration away from the coastal zone, with further stimulation coming about through government and private lending agencies and appropriate tax incentives.

It should be underlined at this point that population control cannot be accomplished by family planning (Davis, 1971). People migrate to have a better life. People marry to have children. Reducing the number of children within a marriage is most difficult for official policy to bring about (Davis, 1971). Influencing movements of people within a country is the more reasonable approach to population management within the coastal zone.

Any policy must be based on the knowledge that the migrants, in general, will come from lower strata of society than that of the indigenous population and will tend to have larger families; this will lead, during early periods, to higher population increases than are desirable.

Recognizing that the lower economic classes make up the bulk of the immigrants to the coastal zone (there are some clearcut exceptions, like the movement of the wealthy Hong Kong residents to more acceptable habitats in the coastal zones of Canada in the face of the handing back of their territory to China), population policies must emphasize an improved social status.

The Mediterranean basin

The Mediterranean basin provides a proving ground for conflicts that most probably will develop between populations of the developed world (the northern countries) and those of the developing world (the southern countries) in coastal zones. Birth rates and death rates of the indigenous populations are obviously two important factors (Grenon and Batisse, 1989) (see Chapter 1). Overall, the local population of the Mediterranean coastal zone will be increasing over the next decades through these parameters alone and will stress existing resources.

But what about international migration to the north brought about by the desire for a higher quality of life by the lower strata of the Mediterranean society, i.e. those in the African countries to the south? Grenon and Batisse (1989) argue that '(international migration)... is so complex that it has to be confined to a few considerations ... in the construction of scenarios'.

Since the 1960s, the European countries have imported unskilled and semi-skilled labourers from adjacent countries to the south and to the east. Grenon and Batisse point out that about half of the foreign population in EEC states is of Mediterranean origin.

But the most deprived are to the south. These citizens seeing a better life on television, in the cinema, on the printed page, etc. especially a better life in countries just separated from their own by a strip of water, will have a strong compulsion to join the migrant force.

Predicting migration patterns is difficult. Clearly, they do not follow regulations imposed by the country of origin or by the country receiving immigrants. They follow the unwritten economic and social incentives of those moving. Some indication of the economic pressures can be seen in the additions to and the withdrawals from the labour markets in the next decade. Whereas in the northern European countries the entries are predicted to be less than the withdrawals beginning about 2015, the entries in the southern countries and Turkey are always higher than the withdrawals up to this year. The search for a better life through better employment may drive the international migration, either clandestine or above-board.

Racial diversity

The racial diversity of immigrants arriving in some coastal zones add to the problems of population management. Often, a large number of refugees fleeing a single country will populate one area of the host country. Since often they do not share the same language, customs and life-styles of the natives of the host country, they tend to find strength in congregating together. Thus, in directing the migrants away from the coastal zone, consideration must be given to their social background if appropriate employment, housing etc. is to be developed.

The State of California is perhaps among the most racially diverse areas both in the United States and perhaps in the world (Table 10.1 and Fullwood, 1991). California's white majority continues to fall from the 1990 census percentage of 69 per cent. This contrasts with the growing Asian population of 7.4 per cent, made up of immigrants from a variety of countries, including the Philippines, Vietnam, Cambodia, the Republic of Korea, Thailand, among others.

The Hispanic migrant population provides the bulk of the agricultural workers, hard working and lowly paid, with often substandard housing. Disputes with the local populations, as well as with governmental agencies, are serious. Those migrants in the coastal zone would welcome, most probably, a chance at a better life elsewhere.

Table 10.1. *California's ethnic makeup as compared to selected other states (Fulwood, 1991)*

State	Total	White	Black	Am. Indian	Asian	Hispanic	Other
California	29,760,021	20,524,327	2,208,801	242,164	2,848,659	7,687,938	3,939,070
New York	17,990,455	13,385,255	2,859,055	62,651	692,760	2,214,026	989,734
Texas	16,986,510	12,774,762	2,021,632	65,877	319,459	4,339,905	1,804,780
Florida	12,937,926	10,749,285	1,759,534	36,335	154,302	1,574,143	238,470
Colorado	3,294,394	2,905,474	133,146	27,776	59,862	424,302	168,136
Mass.	6,016,425	5,405,374	300,130	12,241	143,392	287,549	155,288
Oklahoma	3,145,585	2,583,512	233,801	252,420	33,563	86,160	42,289

Afterword

I began this consideration of the coastal zone with a chapter on population. I close with one. A rising population in this part of our geography threatens the continued development of resources. The world's coastal zones are exits and adits for a mobilized population. The resources of the coastal zone provide a better life for most of its inhabitants and are a lodestone to others. But for an upwardly mobile group the ocean is not a necessary accompaniment to achieve a better lifestyle. For a more effective development of the coastal zone, the most important problem is population management.

References

Davis, Kingsley. The nature and purpose of population policy. *In: California's Twenty Million,* eds. Kingsley Davis and Fredrick G. Styles. Population Monograph Series No. 10. Institute of International Studies, University of California, Berkeley, pp. 3–29 (1971).

Fulwood, S. California is most racially diverse state. *Los Angeles Times,* 13 June (1991).

Grenon, M. and Batisse, M. *Futures for the Mediterranean Basin. The Blue Plan.* Oxford University Press, xviii + 279 p. (1989).